COVER YOUR NUT

PRACTICAL ACCOUNTING IN PLAIN ENGLISH FOR THE REAL WORLD

BY

R.G. BUD PHELPS

Bloomington, IN Milton Keynes, UK

authorHOUSE

AuthorHouse™
1663 Liberty Drive, Suite 200
Bloomington, IN 47403
www.authorhouse.com
Phone: 1-800-839-8640

AuthorHouse™ UK Ltd.
500 Avebury Boulevard
Central Milton Keynes, MK9 2BE
www.authorhouse.co.uk
Phone: 08001974150

First published by AuthorHouse 4/19/2006

ISBN: 1-4259-3509-5 (e)
ISBN: 1-4259-1997-9 (sc)

Library of Congress Control Number: 2006901980

Printed in the United States of America
Bloomington, Indiana

This book is printed on acid-free paper.

657.071
Phe

TABLE OF CONTENTS

INTRODUCTION

ABOUT THE AUTHOR
BY
DON FARRALL

Twenty years ago I started my first business, a commercial photography studio, in Dallas, Texas. I was 25 years old, had a degree in photography, with five years of on-the-job experience working as a staff photographer for a large corporation. I possessed the skills necessary to produce a quality product, but I was clueless when it came to the important task of setting up a meaningful accounting system for my new business. Bud Phelps is my father-in-law, and as such was keenly interested in seeing me succeed in business.

I had a typical business plan; work hard and make lots of money, not too original, and not too big on detail. As I spent time with Bud, I shared my ideas of how my new business would operate. Bud helped me project startup costs, operational costs, revenue, and cash flow; all based on my input and Bud's past business experiences. Bud also introduced me to the concept of "covering your nut", a principal and a phrase that has stuck with me from the first day I was exposed to it.

I also read a book on starting your first business; a book much like this one. Over the years, I have come to appreciate how crucial it is to understand the underlying financial activities that make a business tick.

To succeed in business, a basic understanding of accounting is mandatory, not optional. Meeting state and federal tax requirements alone requires accurate and meaningful record keeping.

When an accounting system is crafted in a manner that yields meaningful data to the business operator then it becomes so much more than record-keeping. This book "Cover Your Nut" outlines in plain english how successful companies have set-up accounting systems that provide valuable insight into the profitable operation of their business.

"Cover Your Nut" is a resource based on accepted accounting principals and on a number of real world business examples. Read it to attain a better grasp of accounting practices. Read it to find inspiration from the behind-the-scene business philosophies outlined in the business examples. When put in to practice, "Cover Your Nut" thinking will keep any business on the right track to success.

INTRODUCTION

ABOUT THE BOOK
BY
R.G. BUD PHELPS

We would all like to be able to magically know which business we should start on our own, which business would make us the most money, which business would be the easiest to control, how we should set up our business to give us all the information that we need, and what details we should cover while planning all of these items, and, most importantly, how do we "Cover Our Nut".

I have been involved in accounting and management for approximately 50 years and luckily have been involved in various different types and styles of businesses. I worked at a public accounting firm while attending college, and therefore had the opportunity to gain experience in general small business accounting and auditing, and also participated in the establishment of a cost system in a manufacturing company. These experiences led me to my first accounting job in a manufacturing company in Colorado, the Jolly Rancher Candy Company. From that point in time, little did I realize that my business experience would include the following: a candy manufacturing company, a cellophane printing company, a snack food company, an interior decorating and furniture sales company, a camper and trailer manufacturing company, a mobile home manufacturing and sales company, a water well drilling company, an ammunition manufacturing company, and a pet product manufacturing and marketing company.

I have also been involved in establishing accounting and cost system programs for many different types of businesses, from a service business to a manufacturing business and several in between.

These experiences have always come back to the very important fact which is the title to this book, "Cover Your Nut".

I will be providing the reader with the basics to building the information in their accounting systems or business plans to accomplish this. The systems can provide the information to assure that all costs are covered; but it is necessary that management not only understand how to read this information, but do so throughout any operating cycle.

Let's get back to the original thought above: what business should I be involved in? I am going to cover several different types of businesses to give the reader an insight into their operations. I will not be using actual companies, but realistic studies based upon actual companies. I will give the reader an outline of the individual business that will include: the type of business, an analysis regarding the business concept, the marketing strategy, and financial information that will cover budgets, forecasts, and break-even analysis, (Will it "Cover Your Nut"?).

All of us would like that magic formula to pick the business that we would like to start and run successfully, and hopefully this book will at least give you some new insights covering the different types of businesses.

All of the businesses that I will review in this book require a planned management level accounting system to assure that all bases are covered as the company goes through each of the operating cycles.

Look at it this way, the item names (accounts), shown on a financial statement are intentionally placed in an order that allows management to read what has happened during an operating cycle (one month, six months, or a year). Keeping track of the company's assets, liabilities, income and expenses is all taken care of by a good accounting system and proper recording of the individual transactions.

My goal in this book is to give you a better understanding of the role of accounting in managing a company and the application of these management skills. I do not intend upon teaching you to become an accountant, but to give you a better understanding of the need for accounting systems in developing your management skills. You can always hire an accountant, but don't you think that it would be in your best interest to develop an understanding of what the financial statements can show you?

In managing your business your goal should be to develop a basic understanding of accounting with the point of being able to read a financial statement presented to you by an accountant. If you do establish this basic understanding; managing the company, planning for expansion, or seeking a credit line from a bank, they will all become easier for you. The manager should be able to tell the accountant what he expects out of his accounting system and financial statements rather than the other way around.

Read this book with the goal to develop the understanding of why you should "Cover Your Nut" in any business!

I have placed the "Glossary of Accounting Terms", at the beginning, just after this introduction, to enable you to review some of the terms used throughout the book before diving into it. This will also position the glossary at a convenient position for a quick reference while you are reading the book, or just when you would like to refer back to it.

GLOSSARY OF ACCOUNTING TERMS

I have used these accounting terms as they are intended to be used throughout this book, but hopefully have also given you the information to better understand them while you are reading this book. I have included this glossary for you readers and potential managers to use as a quick reference guide for those elusive terms you may still have trouble understanding, not only while reading this book but in the future.

Account – can best be defined as a named item used in accounting to record each financial transaction that takes place during an operational period. Example: each balance sheet named account will either be an asset, liability, or equity item (such as; cash, accounts payable-trade, or capital stock), and the income statement named accounts will either be an income or expense item (such as; sales-products or advertising expense). The chart of accounts is a listing of all of the items (accounts) used in recording the company's financial transactions.

Accounting – a system of recording, verifying, and reporting financial transactions.

Accounting period – a unit of time for which revenues and expenses are recorded and reported (months, quarters, and years).

Accounts Payable – the recorded amounts a company owes to other companies and individuals for goods and services received.

Accounts Receivable – the recorded amounts owed a company for goods and services delivered.

Accounts Receivable Turnover – the mathematical ratio used to measure the number of times in an accounting period the company receives the money owed them (total credit sales divided by average accounts receivable).

Accrual basis accounting – the type of accounting required by GAAP for companies to match income with expenses incurred in the same period. (credit sales or services received but not paid for are examples).

Accumulated depreciation – the cumulative depreciation for fixed assets. In other words, it is the accumulation of depreciation from both prior and current periods until the value of the asset is totally expensed.

Amortization – just as in depreciation, amortization is an accounting method used to reduce an intangible asset value over time. Amortization also refers to an amount that reduces the principal of a loan through periodic payments.

Annual Report – the year-end financial statement package which covers the year's operation including: the balance sheet, income statement, cash flow statement, footnotes to the statements, and the auditor's opinion.

Assets – items a company owns that are listed on the balance sheet.

Audit – an objective examination of the company's records, financial statements, and supporting documents to ensure that they have been recorded consistently and conform to GAAP rules.

Balance Sheet – the financial statement or report covering everything the company owns (assets), owes (liabilities), with the difference between the two being equity the breakdown of the owner's investment.   It is based upon the accounting model: Assets = Liabilities + Equity.

Basic Accounting Model – Assets = Liabilities + Equity.

Book Value – the net value of an asset shown on the balance sheet = (asset cost minus depreciation or amortization). This value would be historical cost (or appreciated value) less depreciation.

Break-even Point – is the point at which revenues equal costs; or, as I have said, the point when you "Cover Your Nut".

Budget Report – is a report that covers the estimated revenues and expenses for an extended period of time (one or more years). This report is management's projection of what could happen in future periods.

Business risk – the risk associated with the operation of the business.

Capital appreciation – is the accepted increased value of an asset over its purchase price as referred to under book value.

Capital Stock – is a unit of ownership of a company that can be transferred or sold to another.

Capitalizing the cost – to accumulate cost items of a fixed asset (example: labor and material of a fixed asset manufactured within the company).

Cash Flow Statement – the financial statement detailing where a company's money came from and where it ends up is the cash flow statement. (Examples: money came from profit and was spent on an asset).

Cash on hand – the currency and coins not deposited in the company's bank account is considered petty cash.

Chart of accounts - a listing of all of the items (accounts) used in recording the company's financial transactions

Collateral – something of value pledged as security for a loan.

Contra accounts – contra accounts will have a balance different than what you normally would expect. (Example: an asset having a credit balance would be considered a contra account, such as accumulated depreciation. In this situation, the contra account – accumulated depreciation reduces the value of the asset account.)

Corporation – a legal entity that is separate and apart from its owners. It has limited liability for the owners, easy transfer of ownership (sale of stock), and a continuing existence.

Cost of Good Sold – an item shown on the profit and loss statement that reflects the cost of products (in relation to sales) sold during an accounting cycle.

Cover Your Nut – to cover all costs relative to income. The break-even report shown in this book is a tool used to see at what point in the volume of revenue the company will cover all costs.

Credit – a decrease in assets or expenses or an increase in liabilities, owner's equity, or revenue, example: purchase of an inventory item decreases cash (credit) and increases inventory (debit). I had an accounting instructor that jokingly told our class that credits were the ones closest to the window.

Current Assets – the assets that will be converted to cash within a year.

Current Liabilities – amounts owed by the company that will be paid within a year.

Current Ratio – the ratio mathematically computed by dividing current liabilities into current assets. The weakness in this ratio is, as I pointed out under the review of ratios, inventories are included in current assets and may not be readily converted to cash.

Debit – an increase in assets or expenses or a decrease in liabilities, owner's equity or revenue. Example: receiving a cash payment for an accounts receivable increases cash (debit) and decreases accounts receivable (credit). Remember, debits are not the ones closest to the window.

Depreciation – the reduction of value of a fixed asset over a time frame and shown on the income statement as an expense. The amount to reduce the fixed asset is determined by a defined depreciation method; straight line and double-declining balance are examples of the most common methods used.

Direct Costs – the costs directly related to the production of goods or services.

Direct Labor – the labor costs directly related to the production of goods or services.

Direct Materials – the raw material items directly related to the production of goods.

Dividends – the payments made to stockholders from a corporation's retained earnings or profits. The dividend represents a return on the stockholders' investment.

Double-declining balance (DDB) Depreciation – an accelerated method of depreciation that allows a company to take more depreciation expense earlier in a fixed asset's life. This method is also know as 200% declining balance (DDB) and is an approved expense for federal income tax preparation.

Double-entry bookkeeping – the practice of using debits = credits and assets = liabilities + owners' equity methods to make sure financial transactions are accurately recorded in all entries. Examples: (1) debit cash and credit accounts receivable when a customer pays his invoice. (2) credit sales and debit accounts receivable when recording a sale on account to a customer.

Earnings per share (EPS) – tells the investors in a company how much each share of stock has earned. It is calculated as the net income of the company divided by the average number of outstanding shares of stock.

Equity – the portion of ownership in property. This could be the assets of a company or individuals assets.

Expense – the charges (or reduction) of profit. These are the items necessary for a company's operation and are the accumulated charges against revenue.

FASB – is an independent board (Financial Accounting Standards Board) that outlines accounting practices and (GAAP) Generally Accepted Accounting Principles.

Face value of a loan – the amount shown as the principal balance of the loan.

Federal Reserve – the national banking authority that regulates the U.S. money supply, oversees national monetary policies, and makes sure that national banks are adhering to those policies.

Federal Unemployment Tax Act (FUTA) – the federal law that requires employers to contribute to a government fund, which in turn pays unemployment benefits to individuals who are terminated or laid off.

Finance – the science involving the interpretation of information compiled in accounting, predicting outcomes, and planning to achieve favorable financial results.

Financial Ratios – the comparisons which allow a manager or investor to evaluate how well a company is performing (compared to itself, to competition, and to industry averages).

Financial risk – the relationship to the amount of debt that a company uses to fund its operations.

Financial Statements – the standardized reports (GAAP) prepared to show a company's financial information. Examples: balance sheet, income statement, and statement of cash flow.

Finished Goods – the inventory items that are ready to be sold.

First-in, First-out (FIFO) – an inventory valuation method treating the oldest items in the inventory as the first ones sold.

Fixed Costs – the expenses that are relatively the same, no matter how much a company produces or sells. Examples: rent, utilities, and base salaries.

Float – the difference between the time a check is written and mailed and the time it clears the bank. The new electronic banking laws limit the float time considerably, therefore, the individual must insure that he has a sufficient amount in his bank to cover each check to avoid bank charges. Electronically, the check could clear your bank instantly.

F.O.B. (Free on Board) shipping point – designates that the title of goods passes when the seller delivers the goods to the shipper.

F.O.B. (Free on Board) destination – designates that the title of goods passes when the goods arrive at the customers ship-to address.

Forecasting – the finance tool used to project future revenues, expenses, or major capital expenditures of a company. It is used as a managerial tool to project the company's ability to cover future periods of financial activity.

GAAP (Generally Accepted Accounting Principles) – the Financial Accounting Standards Board established these principles as rules governing accounting practices for financial transactions and reporting statements.

General and Administrative Expenses (G&A) – the expenses related to the administration of the company and not included in the cost of goods sold items.

General Journal – the financial diary of the company covering the transactions (debits and credits) recorded in order by date throughout the year.

General Ledger – the collection of all of the company's financial accounts.

Goodwill – the intangible characteristics of a company. Examples: good reputation, established brand names, and loyal customers. These characteristics can result in more profits and/or increased value of the company.

In the Black – the company is earning a profit.

In the Red – the company is operating at a loss.

Income Statement – the financial statement outlines a company's revenues and expenses for a defined period of time in a report format. It is formally known as the statement of income for a specific period of time (month, quarter, or year).

Indirect Costs – labor costs that are not directly involved in the manufacturing process; such as salaries, wages, and related expenses for supervisors, managers, janitors, or engineers.

Inflation Rate – the percentage increase that prices are rising over a definite period of time.

Intangible Assets – the company assets that are listed on the balance sheet – Examples: goodwill or patents.

Interest – the amount paid to a lender for the use of its money.

Interest Rate – the percentage charged (or paid) for the use of money.

Journal Entry – the recording of financial transactions in the general journal utilizing debits and credits.

Last-in, First-out (LIFO) – an inventory valuation method. When inventory is sold, this method treats the last item purchased as the first item sold.

Leasehold Improvements – this is the accounting of costs accumulated when improvements to a leasehold property will have a depreciable life of more than one year.

Liabilities – the amounts a company owes to other businesses or individuals.

Lien – the public record a lender has filed giving him first priority over the property pledged as collateral by the company if the debt is not paid.

Limited Liability Corporation (LLC) – a company that is a cross between a sole proprietorship/partnership and a corporation. It allows the members to be protected from liability for debts incurred by the entity, but doesn't have the extensive reporting requirements of a corporation. Like a sole proprietorship/ partnership, they do have a limited life.

Line item – an individual account on a financial statement.

Liquid Assets – assets that can be quickly converted to cash.

Liquidation Value – the cash value that can be generated as a result of selling all the assets of a company.

Liquidity Ratios – mathematically computed ratios that reflect a company's ability to pay its current debt. The two ratios are: (1) current ratio – the most common (current assets divided by current liabilities) and (2) quick ratio – (usually = current assets minus inventory divided by current liabilities, as inventory isn't always easily converted to cash).

Loan Agreement – the legal contract containing all the terms and conditions of the loan.

Loan Amortization Schedule – the spreadsheet or financial statement that details the portion of each payment which reduces the principal or becomes the interest. The schedule can be preprinted showing the principal and interest payments when made on a specific day, or can be computed relative to the days outstanding between payments for each individual payment.

Loan Closing – the meeting resulting the final signing of the loan agreements by both the lender and the borrower.

Loan Payoff – the amount required to pay off the loan at a given point in time. The payoff will include the remaining principal, as well as the interest due at that point in time.

Long Term Assets – the assets that have an estimated useful life of more than one year.

Long Term Liabilities – the liabilities that will come due longer than a one year time frame.

Lower of Cost or Market (LCM) – a GAAP rule regarding your inventory value; if the market value decreases below recorded value, the inventory must be written down to this lower value.

Manufacturing Overhead – an amount that covers all costs related to the manufacturing process of products except direct material and direct labor.

Net Income – the result of revenues exceeding expenses incurred to generate the revenues.

Net Loss – the result of expenses exceeding revenues in a given period of time.

Notes Payable – the promissory notes made by the company or an individual to pay a certain amount of money with interest on specific due dates.

Operating Capital – the monies a company uses to operate from day to day.

Outstanding Stock – the company's stock that is held by others.

Owner's Equity – the same as stockholder's equity, however, this term usually applies to sole proprietorships, whereas stockholder's equity applies to corporations. In either situation, equity is the ownership portion of the company.

Paid-in Capital – the amounts paid for stock above the stated par value. Example: paying $5 for stock that has $1 par value would result in paid-in capital of $4.

Par Value – the face value or stated value of a security as it appears on the certificate.

Partnership – a type of company organization comprised of two or more owners who are equally liable for issues associated with the company and are known as general partnerships. Limited partnerships are as stated, limited in control and/or liability.

Payback Period – a term relative to the length of time it will take a company to earn back its initial investment in a project.

Payroll Bank Account – the account established exclusively for the payroll payments.

Payroll Taxes – the employer's portion of FICA and Medicare that are paid to the Social Security Administration for their employees.

Pension Plan – the systematic accumulation and investment of money by the company for the purpose of providing retirement benefits for its employees.

Periodic Inventory – an established program to physically count inventories at specific timeframes. The physical count allows accountants to adjust inventory values to the actual counts. The adjustment to the actual count allows the valuation on the balance sheet to be corrected to true counts on hand, rather than unadjusted running balances.

Personal Guarantee – a signed guarantee by the owner that a debt will be repaid, even if the company goes into default. Banks or other lenders may require this type of guarantee because of the limited liability of a corporation.

Petty Cash – the small amount of cash on hand, perhaps $100-$500 a company has to purchase miscellaneous items.

Posting – the act of recording general journal transactions into the general ledger. Posting in the past was a hand operation, but now most of the posting is accomplished automatically as transactions are entered on a computer through the accounting software program.

Preferred Stock – a class of stock that defines one or more preferences over common stock, such as a right to pay a specific dividend before common stockholders.

Prepaid Expenses – expenses that have been paid in advance of receiving the benefit of the goods or services. Example: insurance, trip expenses, or postage meter refills.

Price Earnings Ratio (PE) – the mathematical computation of the relationship between stock price and earnings. The formula for PE is the current market price per share of stock divided by earnings per share.

Prime Rate – the current interest rate a lending institution charges its best customers.

Principal – the balance of money borrowed by the company for a specific note or the stated value (or face value) of a bond.

Private Accountant – how an accountant is classified when he works for a company rather than for an accounting firm.

Profit & Loss Statement – the same as the income statement of a company.

Profitability Ratios – the ratios that measure performance as indicated by a company's return on sales or assets. The common profitability ratios are: gross profit margin (GPM), net profit margin (NPM), return on assets (ROA), return on equity (ROE), return on sales (ROS), and return on investment (ROI).

Property & Real Estate Taxes – the taxes paid to local, county, or state governments as a privilege to do business in their area.

Public Accountant – how an accountant is classified when he works for an accounting firm.

<u>Quick Assets</u> – the assets that are easily converted to cash; current assets minus inventory.

<u>Quick Ratio</u> – the liquidity ratio of assets that are easily converted to cash; current assets minus inventory divided by current liabilities = quick ratio.

<u>Raw Materials</u> – the inventory items that must be processed before they can be sold as finished goods.

<u>Reconcile an Account</u> – the process that compares an account balance with an independent source (such as a bank statement), where adjustments for errors and omissions can be made.

<u>Retained Earnings</u> – the account which records the accumulation of earnings, less payments of dividends to stockholders since inception of the company.

<u>Revenues (Sales)</u> – the income received for sales of products or services.

<u>Sales Discounts</u> – the allowances or markdowns from the original selling prices of products.

<u>Sales Returns & Allowances</u> – the account showing the amounts given back to customers for items returned for credit.

<u>Servicing Debt</u> – the act of keeping both the principal and interest payments current, that are due on a note.

<u>Share</u> – one unit of a company's ownership.

<u>Shareholders</u> – also known as stockholders and represents the individuals or legal entities that own stock in a company.

<u>Short-term Forecast</u> – a forecast done mid-year to predict expenses and revenues for the balance of the year.

Simple Interest – the interest calculated on the principal amount of the loan only, equals principal times interest times time.

Sole Proprietorship – a business in which one person owns the company. That one person is the business entity for federal income tax purposes.

State Unemployment Tax Act (SUTA) – the state law that requires employers to contribute to a state government fund that pays unemployment benefits to people who are terminated or laid off.

Stock Certificates – printed or engraved documents that are evidence that a stockholder owns shares of the company's stock.

Subchapter S Corporation (S Corp) – a classification that allows corporate earnings to be taxed on the owners' federal income tax return, thereby eliminating the problem of double taxation. The c corporation is taxed on the profits, and the individual stockholder is taxed on the dividends.

Sum-of-the-Years' Digits (SYD) – an accelerated method of depreciation that allows a company to record more depreciation early in a fixed asset's life.

T-Account – an accounting tool used to chart financial transactions. The idea is to put a T on a scratch pad with an account name written on the top, inserting the debit entries on the left and the credit entries on the right to easily trace a transaction.

T accounts are easy tools for quick analysis of an account, and can help the manager better understand the accounting footprints!

Tangible Assets – assets that you can see and touch, such as buildings or furniture and equipment.

TOWS Review – this review is utilized when making an analysis of a business, and consists of the following:

> Threats – what known and unknown threats are against the business?
>
> Opportunities – what opportunities appear to be available for the business?
>
> Weaknesses – what weaknesses appear that could be a detriment to success?
>
> Strengths – what are the obvious strengths of the business?

Treasury Stock – stock that a company buys back from stockholders.

Unsecured Debt – debt that is not supported by collateral (assets).

Useful Life – the period of time you expect an asset to be usable.

Variable Costs – costs that can increase or decrease depending on the level of sales or production.

Work In Progress – also know as work in process and both terms refer to partially completed manufactured products in inventory.

Yield – the percentage return on an investment.

Section 1 – Accounting 101

1.1 Accounting and Business Questions and Answers

1.2 Basic Accounting Information

1.3 Accounting Footprints

1.1 - ACCOUNTING AND BUSINESS QUESTIONS WITH ANSWERS

01 - DO I HAVE WHAT IT TAKES TO OWN/MANAGE A SMALL BUSINESS?

You will be your own most important employee, so an objective appraisal of your strengths and weaknesses is essential. Some questions you should ask yourself are:

- ➢ **Am I a self-starter?**
- ➢ **How good am I at making decisions?**
- ➢ **How well do I plan and organize?**
- ➢ **Am I willing to make sacrifices?**
- ➢ **How will I handle stress?**

You are the only one who can answer these questions, but having a better understanding of accounting will certainly help you in the area of making decisions, planning and organizing. In this book, I will cover the basic accounting areas that you should study and understand to help you in your decisions.

02 – WHICH BUSINESS SHOULD I CHOOSE?

Usually the best business for you is the one in which you are the most skilled and interested in. Review your options, consult local experts and businessmen, and then match your background with the local market. Consider working for someone else in a similar business to see how they operate. In this book, I will review several different types of businesses, and this may help in your selection. Remember, you will be the one responsible for these ventures; therefore, make sure that your selection fits your skills and interests.

03 – What is a business plan, and why do I need one?

A business plan precisely defines your business, identifies your goals and serves as your firm's resume. Its basic components include a current balance sheet, an income statement, and a cash flow statement. If you are starting a new business, some of the information in your initial statements will have to be presented in the form of projections. The data should be based on credible assumptions to be fair to yourself and to anyone else who may be evaluating your business.

The business plan helps you allocate resources properly, handle unforeseen complications, and make the right decisions. Because a business plan provides specific and organized information about your company and how you will repay borrowed money, a good business plan is a crucial part of any loan package. Additionally, it can tell your sales personnel, suppliers and others about your operations and goals.

This book has not been written just for the development of a business plan, but will give you the understanding of the statements required and the reasons for planned management financial statements.

04 – What do I need to succeed in a business?

The basic items that you need for successes in a business are:

➢ **Sound management practices**
➢ **Industry experience**
➢ **Technical support**
➢ **Planning ability**
➢ **Investment capital**
➢ **Stamina / endurance**

Few people start a business with all of these bases covered. You must honestly assess your own experience and skills and assure that you have partners or key employees who can compensate for your deficiencies.

This book will attempt to give you an understanding of the skills necessary for sound accounting practices along with the development of managerial financial statements.

05 – DO I NEED A COMPUTER AND TELECOMMUNICATION EQUIPMENT?

Computers can assist the small businessman in general accounting and inventory controls, and give managers the tools to better measure the effectiveness of their activities in the company's operations. Business and accounting software programs (such as QuickBooks) can be customized to fit the specific needs of and type of business. These programs can be very beneficial to give management quick reports from the accumulated transactions and through the customized listing of the chart of accounts.

Telecommunication equipment (phones, fax machines and network connections) are necessary for all common business functions: sales, purchasing, financing, operations and administration.

This book will assist the reader in establishing the key accounting information before starting the business computer programs, supplying tools toward the development of better financial statements.

06 – HOW MUCH MONEY DO I NEED TO GET STARTED?

The determination of how much money will depend upon the direction that you plan to take your company and the items you will need to cover, such as:

- ➢ **The building and equipment needs**
- ➢ **The beginning inventory needs**
- ➢ **The money available to cover operating expenses for at least a year (Includes your salary, money to repay loans, and general start up expenses).**

07 – WHAT ARE THE ALTERNATIVES IN FINANCING A BUSINESS?

First, you need the commitment of your own funds; this will become the indicator of how serious you are about your business. You may want to seek out investors that also believe in your idea for this business venture. Banks are an obvious source of funds, but you must be properly prepared with a good business plan before you approach financing institutions. Banks are not in the venture capital risk business; they will not lend funds without sufficient collateral to back up the loan. Banks will help you in the preparation of an SBA loan package and advise you of your best approach, but more than likely will not lend funds for a start-up company unless your individual collateral covers the loan. Other loan sources: are commercial finance companies, venture capital firms, local development companies, and life insurance companies.

This book will assist the reader in establishing the key financial statements necessary for the preparation of a good business plan to secure financing.

08 – WHAT KIND OF PROFITS CAN I EXPECT?

This is not an easy question. Profit is the funds left over after all expenses (from cost of goods through all expenses including your salary) are taken care of. There are standards of comparison called "industry ratios" which can help you estimate the profits you can expect and will need. Return on your original investment estimates the amount of profit gained on a given number of dollars invested in the business. These ratios are broken down by standard industrial classification (SIC) code and size, so you can look up your type of business to see what the industry averages are. These figures are published by several groups, and can be found at your library. Help is also available through the SBA and the trade associations that serve your industry.

This book will give you some examples of businesses along with their concepts, marketing plans, and some financial information about each company reviewed.

09 – What should I know about accounting and bookkeeping?

As you will see in this book, I feel very strongly about your need to know as much as you can about accounting and bookkeeping. Accounting and bookkeeping dates back before Roman times, and I feel that the need for it will continue as long as there are business operations to measure.

Accounting and bookkeeping are the footprints leading you to what has happened economically to your business. Therefore, a manager needs to know how to follow these footprints. I will give you these footprint finders throughout this book to aid in the development of your system.

A manager needs to know the rules, such as: Generally Accepted Accounting Principles (GAAP) which I will go over in the next section. How could a manager really know his business if he didn't have some basic understanding of accounting and bookkeeping?

10 – How do I set up my accounting and bookkeeping system?

If you supply the input for setting up your accounting system, it will be a much more meaningful and useful program for you, and the financial statements will become management statements. Some of the things that you should consider before setting up your accounting and bookkeeping systems are the following:

- ➢ **How will the records be used?**
- ➢ **How important is this information likely to be?**
- ➢ **Is the information available elsewhere?**
- ➢ **Will you need management, or investment, or credit statements?**
- ➢ **What level of detail should be tracked?**
- ➢ **How can the information be of the most use to me?**

11 – What financial statements will I need?

You should plan for three kinds of statements:

> **Standard balance sheet (comparative when information is available)**
> **Income statement (comparative when information is available)**
> **Cash flow statement (where cash came from and where it went)**

I will cover the rules regarding financial statements established through applying, Generally Accepted Accounting Principles (GAAP). The next section will give you the details regarding these principles and teach you how to read and understand them.

12 – What does "Cover Your Nut" mean?

The "Cover Your Nut" principle means that your sales and revenue must cover all of your costs and expenses over a given time frame. Another way of putting it is your "break-even point", the sales and revenue level where you cover all costs and expenses for a specific period (month, quarter, or year). To establish a "Cover Your Nut" report or a "break-even" report you will need the following information:

> **What are your projected sales and revenue?**
> **What are your fixed expenses?**
> **What are your variable costs?**

Projected sales and revenue is the listing of all sources of income available to you. Examples: product sales, rental income, interest income.

Fixed expenses are the expenses that remain constant over the period covered. Examples: general insurance, rent, base telephone bill, and depreciation.

Variable Costs are the costs that change as sales and revenue change. Examples: sales commissions, shipping costs, and insurance relative to sales.

There are many more questions you may think of, but I feel that after reading this book many of your questions will be answered. My goal in writing this book is to teach the reader what he should know about any company he may be involved with. I have found over the years that it really doesn't matter what type of business you have because all businesses have cash requirements, employee requirements, marketing requirements, facility requirements, supply requirements, and, most importantly, management requirements.

If you are involved in a manufacturing company (it really doesn't matter what you are making), each item that you produce requires material, labor to put it together, and supplies to make it happen. Then advertising and marketing are needed to create the demands for the product, and shipping supplies and shipping companies are also needed to move the product to its destination. All of these items require a management accounting system to record all of the individual transactions, and finally, financial statements to measure the effectiveness of the company's operation. I was involved in a manufacturing company that made candy, which required sugar, corn syrup, and flavoring as some its ingredients; also, a manufacturing company that made ammunition, which required powder, primers, cartridge cases, and bullets as some of its components; both needed equipment and labor to put the materials together.

Manufacturing companies naturally are more complicated because of all of the steps necessary to produce a product. These complications require more diligence in the development of the accounting systems.

If you are involved in a company that sells a product it doesn't really matter how different it is from a manufacturing company, it still needs sales of products, sales salaries, sacks or boxes, general supplies, advertising and marketing. It also needs the accounting system to record all of the transactions that will give you the information to prepare the financial statements. Knowing at what point in time you "Cover Your Nut" can be very important.

We all would like that magic crystal ball that would answer all of our questions, but when you get right down to it, the requirements are simple. You must carefully prepare all of the information about your proposed venture to find the answers. Will it really work? You must be diligent in the collection of this information and not expect to have the answers without the input of all of the key information.

Watch for the footprints throughout this book that will guide you in making your final decisions.

1.2 - BASIC ACCOUNTING PRINCIPLES

ACCOUNTING AND THE "COVER YOUR NUT PRINCIPLE"

Accounting is here to stay; it started before the Roman era and will undoubtedly be here for as long in the future, so let's make it easier to understand and use. I want to show you that accounting is really a ten letter word – not a four letter word like some people call it or think about it. Accounting is a system for recording and measuring the results of an economic activity. Accounting gives us the information that we need to plan for the future, utilizing the information from the past. We can then use this information for the establishment of operating budgets. The results of the application of accounting information through budgets give us the guidelines to set product prices, plan for purchasing or building of materials, and planning for increases in future individual expense items based on historical facts rather than flip-a-coin guesses.

In this section (Accounting 101), I will try to lay the groundwork, for a better understanding of the areas in accounting where many businessmen need the most help. You must understand that the only reason that you are starting a business is to make money, and to do so you must have the tools to accomplish this. "Cover Your Nut" is a general term for covering the costs and expenses of your business to make a profit, and something that is often left out in the early planning stages of a business. In order to make money with your business, the first step should be to see at what point in time, and with what revenue, will I cover all of my costs and expenses. The "Cover Your Nut Principle" is the most important step that you can make toward being successful in reaching that original goal for starting a business, (making money).

THE RULES – GAAP

Accounting follows rules known as Generally Accepted Accounting Principles (GAAP). The Securities & Exchange Commission (SEC), and the Financial Accounting Standards Board (FASB) sets accounting policy in the United States and developed this set of rules called (GAAP).

The rules are made to establish uniformity in accounting systems and financial statements. The following is an example of accounting rules dealing with the basic accounting formula: Assets = Liabilities + Owner's Equity.

In the glossary there is a definition of debits and credits, but the application of these debits and credits can best be understood by applying them to this basic accounting formula.

Again, I am not trying to turn all of the readers into bookkeepers or accountants, but to give them a better understanding of how the information got there.

In a double entry system of accounting, every debit must have an offset entry of a credit; therefore, I feel you should have a better understanding of how the debits and credits apply to this accounting formula. The following examples should give you a better understanding:

Assets	=	Liabilities + Owners Equity
Debit		Credit
Normal debit balance		Normal credit balance
Debits increase asset accounts.		Credits increase liabilities/equity.
Credits decrease asset accounts.		Debits decrease liabilities/equity.

As is shown above, assets normally have debit balances while liabilities and owners equity normally have credit balances. Accounts have two sides, like a **T**; the debits are on the left of the **T** and the credits on the right. **T accounts** are used by accountants as tools to quickly trace the two sides of an entry. I am going to give you several examples of accounts with some balances and entries to give you a better picture. Follow the individual transactions through each account:

12

(1)   Purchase inventory on credit/accounts payable
(2)   Sell inventory on credit and show the sales account
(3)   Collect accounts receivable/cash
(4)   Pay cash for the inventory/accounts payable
(5)   Show the cost of the inventory as cost of goods
(6)   Show profit to retained earnings

Asset - Inventory

	Debit-left	Credit-right	Balance
Beg Bal	$1,000.00		$1,000.00
1	$500.00		$1,500.00
5		$500.00	

Sales

	Debit-left	Credit-right	Balance
2		$750.00	-$750.00
6	$750.00		$0.00

Liabilities - Accounts Payable

	Debit-left	Credit-right	Balance
Beg Bal		$1,200.00	-$1,200.00
1		$500.00	-$1,700.00
4	$1,700.00		$0.00

Cost of Goods			
	Debit-left	Credit-right	Balance
5	$500.00		$500.00
6		$500.00	$0.00

Asset - A/C Recievable			
	Debit-left	Credit-right	Balance
2	$750.00		$750.00
3		$750.00	$0.00

Profit to Retained Earnings			
	Debit-left	Credit-right	Balance
6		$750.00	-$750.00
6	$500.00		-$250.00

Asset - Cash			
	Debit-left	Credit-right	Balance
Beg Bal	$3,000.00		$3,000.00
3	$750.00		$3,750.00
4		$1,700.00	$2,050.00

By following the numbers shown in each account you can easily trace the individual transactions, and in all accounts the debit is on the left and the credit is on the right. Trace the numbers in the example accounts as follows:

1. $500, increase inventory and increase accounts payable
2. $750, increase sales and increase accounts receivable
3. $750, increase cash and decrease accounts receivable
4. $1,700, decrease cash and decrease accounts payable
5. $500, decrease inventory and increase cost of goods
6. $750 debit sales (close), $500 credit cost of goods (close), balance Profit $250

T accounts are easy tools for quick analysis of an account, and can help the manager better understand the accounting footprints! The idea is to put a **T** on a scratch pad with an account name written on the top, inserting the debit entries on the left and the credit entries on the right, to easily trace a transaction. If you look closely at the asset-cash example shown above you can plainly see the **T**. The name of account shown on the top of the **T** is cash, debits on the left of the **T** show, (beginning balance of $3,000 and entry #3 $750), and credits on the right of the **T** show, (entry #4 $1,700). Now it's your turn to try it! (As they say, "Try it, you'll like it"). Pick up a scratch pad and put the information that I just detailed for you using a **T**. Put the name on the top and the entries as stated and you will have your first **T** account. Believe me, it is the quickest tool to plan transactions before you actually post them into your records, reducing entry errors.

Even though I have been an accountant for years, I find myself utilizing the **T** accounts to quickly explain a transaction because it is so much easier for an individual to understand. When you can see where the dollars are going through the accounts, it just is easier to comprehend even the most complex accounting problems.

The Generally Accepted Accounting Principles (GAAP) suggest the use of both historical costs and accrual accounting to measure economic activity and to establish a chart of accounts, utilizing the proper numbering system. Historical costs are the values entered through accounting when a transaction is completed. A transaction records value between accounts in the accounting system, and historical costs recorded in companies' books do not change when market values increase (if market values decrease, then adjustments in book values may be necessary). In the above example of the purchase of inventory this was at historical cost, even if the inventory value changed after the purchase.

Accrual accounting is when transactions are completed and where cash may not be required. A simple example of an accrual is utilities used but not paid for, resulting in an accounts payable due the utility company. An example of accrual accounting was also shown in the examples above (items 1 and 2), buying inventory on credit and selling items to someone on credit.

GAAP requires a numerical system for the development of a chart of accounts relative to the individual account's relationship to the financial statements. The following chart of accounts has been provided as a general example. As stated earlier, each "account" is a specific financial category item.

GAAP utilizes prefix numbers that assist in the orderly placement of the individual items in a financial statement. Some accounting software systems do not require numbers, but without a numerical system the individual items would be listed alphabetically. If the accounts were listed alphabetically in the chart of accounts shown below, you would have accounts receivable first and then buildings with cash showing up third. The numbering system allows the manager to place the individual accounts (items) in the order that he wants them to appear on the financial statement. When you reach the point in this section where I discuss the balance sheet and the income statement, you will see the reason behind the numbering system.

CHART OF ACCOUNTS EXAMPLE:

<u>Current Assets</u>
- 101 – Cash in Bank
  - 101A – Cash in Bank – Checking
  - 101B – Cash in Bank – Savings
  - 101C – Cash in Bank – Money Market
- 110 – Accounts Receivable – Trade
  - 110A – Allowance for Doubtful Accounts
- 111 – Accounts Receivable – Officers
- 112 – Accounts Receivable – Other
- 120 – Inventory Assets
  - 120A – Inventory Assets – Raw Material
  - 120B – Inventory Assets – Work in Process
  - 120C – Inventory Assets – Finished Goods
- 131 – Notes Receivable – Officers
- 132 – Notes Receivable – Other
- 140 – Prepaid Items
  - 140A – Prepaid Insurance
  - 140B – Prepaid Advertising
  - 140C – Prepaid Dues & Fees
  - 140D – Prepaid Office Supplies
  - 140E – Prepaid Trip & Show Expenses
  - 140F – Prepaid Postage

<u>Fixed Assets</u>
- 151 – Buildings
  - 151A – Accumulated Depreciation – Buildings
- 153 – Product Molds
  - 153A – Accumulated Depreciation – Product Molds
- 154 – Office Equipment
  - 154A – Accumulated Depreciation – Office Equipment
- 155 – Landscaping & Fencing
  - 155A – Accumulated Depreciation – Landscaping & Fencing
- 156 – Land

<u>Other Assets</u>
- 161 – Incorporation Expenses
  - 161A – Accumulated Amortization – Incorporation Expenses

<u>Current Liabilities</u>
- 200 – Accounts & Notes Payable Short Term
  - 201 – Accounts Payable – Trade
  - 202 – Accounts Payable – Officers
  - 203 – Accounts Payable – Other
  - 204 – Notes Payable Bank – Short Term
- 210 – Taxes Payable
  - 211 – FICA – Payroll Withholding Taxes Payable
  - 212 – Federal Income Taxes – Payroll Withholding Payable
  - 213 – State Income Taxes – Payroll Withholding Payable
  - 214 – Federal Unemployment Taxes Payable
  - 215 – State Unemployment Taxes Payable
  - 216 – State Sales Taxes Payable

217 – Taxes Property
220 – Payroll Items
    221 – Accrued Payroll
    222 – Workmen's Compensation Insurance Payable
    223 – Health Insurance – Payroll Withholding Payable
230 – Other Payables
    231 – General Insurance Payable
    232 – Trip & Show Expenses Payable

Long Term Liabilities

240 – Notes Payable – Long Term
241 - Notes Payable Bank
    241A – Less Notes Payable Bank – Short Term
242 – Notes Payable Officers

Equity

301 – Capital Stock - Common
    301A – Less Treasury Stock
302 – Paid In Capital
    Retained Earnings
401 – Product Sales
    401A – Sales – Product One
    401B – Sales – Product Two
    401C – Sales – Product Three
    401D – Sales – Product Four
    401E – Sales – Product Five
    401F – Sales – All Other Products
402 – Other Income
    402A – Interest Income
    402B – Lease & Rental Income
    402C – Miscellaneous Income
500 – Cost of Goods Sold
    501 – Material Costs
    502 – Labor Costs
    503 – Freight-out Costs
    504 – Overhead Costs
    505 – Sales Discounts Allowed
    506 – Insurance – Product Liability
600 – Warehouse Operating Expenses
    601 – Shipping Supplies
    602 – Rent Warehouse
    603 – Rent Equipment
    604 – Equipment Repairs
    605 – Building & Grounds Maintenance
    606 – Insurance
        606A – Insurance – Building
        606B – Insurance – Contents
        606C – Insurance – Equipment
    607 – Utilities – Gas & Electric
    608 – Taxes – Personal Property
    609 – Depreciation
        609A – Depreciation – Buildings
        609B – Depreciation – Landscaping & Fencing

609C – Depreciation – Product Molds

700 – Selling Expenses
- 701 – Advertising
    - 701A – Advertising – Media
    - 701B – Advertising – Promotion
    - 701C – Advertising – Samples
    - 701D – Advertising – Direct Mail & Catalogs
    - 701E – Advertising – Agency Costs
- 702 – Trip & Show Expenses
    - 702A – Show Booth Expenses
    - 702B – Trip Expenses - Travel
    - 702C – Trip Expenses – Rental &Auto Expenses
    - 702D – Trip Expenses – Lodging
    - 702E – Trip Expenses – Meals
    - 702F – Trip Expenses – Entertainment
    - 702G – Trip Expenses – Supplies
- 703 – Commissions
- 704 – Telephone
- 705 – Merchant Charges for Credit Card Charges
- 706 – Miscellaneous Selling Expenses

800 – Administration Expenses
- 801 – Salaries – Office
- 802 – Salaries – Officers
- 803 – Payroll Tax Expense – Administration
- 804 – Interest Expenses
- 805 – Insurance Administration
    - 805A – Insurance – General
    - 805B – Insurance – Liability
    - 805C – Insurance – Health & Accident
    - 805D – Insurance – Officer's Life
- 806 – Supplies – Office
- 807 – Professional Fees
    - 807A – Professional Fees – Accounting
    - 807B – Profession Fees – Legal
- 808 – Office Equipment Repairs
- 809 – Postage Expenses
    - 809A – Postage Expenses – General
    - 809B – Postage Expenses – Rentals
- 810 – Licenses, Permits, & Fees
- 811 – Bank Service Charges
- 812 – Contributions
- 813 – Dues & Subscriptions
- 814 – Taxes General
    - 814A – Taxes – Personal Property
    - 814B – Taxes – State Occupation
    - 814C – Taxes – Federal Income Taxes
    - 814D – Taxes – State Income Taxes
    - 814E – Taxes – City & State Sales Taxes
- 815 – Depreciation & Amortization
    - 815A – Depreciation – Office Equipment
    - 815B – Amortization of Incorporation Expenses

Now that your eyes are glazed over from looking at the many numbers in the chart of accounts that I presented to you, let's break them down a little so you can better understand the merit of this venture.

You will see that there is a method to the madness of this extensive chart of accounts. The numbering system is the key that opens the door for developing managerial financial statements.

KEYS BEHIND THE NUMBERS

The lower numbers in the balance sheet (100-140) are all of the current asset accounts that either are already cash or will turn into cash in a short period of time. The current asset accounts are classified as liquid relative to the time frame necessary to turn them into cash.

Cash accounts usually show bank accounts separately, as well as cash on hand (petty cash). Cash accounts should be reconciled monthly to assure all entries have been recorded properly and to avoid banking problems.

Accounts receivable accounts usually have a separation between trade accounts and other receivables shown. Accounts receivable accounts should be aged monthly, with emphasis placed upon establishing reserves for doubtful accounts as they occur, or through a standardized monthly journal entry. Collection efforts made early can save obvious monies for a company.

The inventory accounts can either be shown very simply or with a detailed separation as to the type of inventory. The company must develop standardized systems for inventory control, either through computer programs or manual posting of inventory items. Inventories need to be checked physically to give the manager the same type of reconciling program used for cash (physical counts will assure that the entries have been recorded properly during the period). Normally, physical inventories are taken either semi-annually or annually, and need to be controlled through the establishment of inventory teams selected by management.

Prepaid accounts are the advance payment of some type of expense, and are usually amortized monthly through standard journal entries. The most common prepaid expense accounts would be for insurance, advertising, annual dues and fees, or trip and show expenses.

The accounts (150-160) in this particular chart are the longer term or other assets. This group of accounts includes both the fixed assets as well as the other assets owned by the company.

Fixed asset accounts normally would be the land, buildings, shop equipment, office furniture and fixtures, and leaseholds that are used over an extended period of time. Fixed asset accounts are recorded at historical cost and changed only if large appreciations in values occur. Changes in appreciated values require footnotes to the balance sheet. Depreciation of the fixed assets is normally taken care of with standard journal entries, developed from various fixed asset worksheets, covering the life of the asset as well as the type of depreciation used. The depreciation will become an expense on the income statement, and will add to the accumulated depreciation accounts on the balance sheet.

Other asset accounts usually include common items, such as, the cost of incorporating the company which will be amortized over a reasonable period of time (shown as amortization expense on the income statement and accumulated amortization on the balance sheet).

The accounts 201-232 represent the current liabilities that must be paid the soonest, starting with the lowest number group. The 240's in this case represent the long term debt, and as you can see, we have established accounts to take out the current portion of debt that is due to be paid within a one year time frame.

Accounts payable accounts are shown and named as to their type of account, as an example: Accounts Payable-Trade, Accounts Payable-Officers, and Accounts Payable-Others. These accounts also need to be analyzed monthly to insure that payments are being made properly and available discounts are taken when the financial condition of the company allows. The importance of the company's credit record is obvious.

Notes payable accounts are shown on a current due basis, and usually are separated between the notes due short-term and the notes due long-term, with accounts established for the current portion of long-term notes.

The 300 accounts represent owner's equity and include the stock accounts and the retained earnings accounts.

Capital stock accounts usually will show the separation of stock accounts by type (common or preferred) and by value.

Treasury stock accounts represent buy-back stock that has been purchased by the company from stockholders.

Paid-in capital accounts are established if the company wants to show a difference in the value of the stock versus the amount paid for the stock. Example: if the stock was sold at par value of $1 per share therefore 1,000 shares would be shown as $1,000 and if the par value stock was sold at $1.50 per share - $1,000 would be shown as capital stock and $500 would be show as paid-in capital.

The retained earnings account is the accumulation of profits or losses and may show the profit or loss for the current year as a separate item on the balance sheet.

The numbering system for the income statement has a specific plan: the 400 accounts represent Income, the 500 accounts represent cost of goods sold, the 600 accounts represent operating overhead, the 700 accounts represent selling expenses, and the 800 accounts represent administrative expenses. Within each grouping, the chart of accounts has been expanded to give the manager a more complete insight as to where the income or expenses are coming from.

When a manager becomes familiar with the grouping of the income statement accounts, he has a management tool that will give him trends for his business. It will also allow him to plan much better for the future operation of his company when preparing his budgets. See an example of the income statement later in this section.

The magic in the financial statements is really not magic but common sense. A manager that develops his skills at reading the statements will become a much stronger manager, and will be more aware of what is happening with his company. When he talks to; investors, creditors, or must go to the bank to establish his line of credit, his skills at reading his own statements will go a long way in proving his knowledge of what is happening economically with his company. The results will be a better response from whatever group of people he is meeting with.

The following are examples of the numbering groups in the income statement. I have shown this grouping of the accounts to give you the footprints that will help you in making management analysis of the income statements that you read.

- ➢ **The 400's represent the income accounts**
- ➢ **The 500's represent the cost of goods accounts**
- ➢ **The 600's represent the operating expense accounts**
- ➢ **The 700's represent the selling expense accounts**
- ➢ **The 800's represent the administration expense accounts**

After you have read income statements over an extended period of time, you will be able to see the patterns that are developed in an individual operation. This development of visible patterns indicates the manager's development of footprint guides, for reading the financial statements.

THE BALANCE SHEET

The balance sheet is a snap-shot of the company's assets, liabilities, and owner's equity at a particular point in time, and will be different the very next day. Usually the balance sheet is prepared monthly, quarterly, or annually, and is compared to the balance sheet that was prepared at the same point in time as last month, last quarter, or last year. It really tells you a story about what has happened economically to the company. The reader can now look over the balance sheet and have a better understanding of why the accounts are in a certain position on this financial statement. The following is an example of a balance sheet utilizing some of the numbers in our chart of accounts example, simplified for example purposes, but covering all of the basic items in a standard Balance Sheet.

Balance Sheet Example			
As of October 31, 2005			1 OF 2
ASSETS			
Current Assets			
101A Cash in Bank - Checking	$15,550.00		
101B Cash in Bank - Savings	$5,300.00		
Total Cash in Bank		$20,850.00	
110 Accounts Receivable Trad	$16,000.00		
110A Allowance for Doubtful	-$320.00		
Total Receivables		$15,680.00	
120A Inventory - Raw Materia	$5,750.00		
120C Inventory - Finished Go	$60,230.00		
Total Inventory		$65,980.00	
140A Prepaid Insurance	$5,780.00		
140B Prepaid Advertising	$2,500.00		
140C Prepaid Dues & Fees	$1,250.00		
140E Prepaid Trip & Show Ex	$5,000.00		
Total Prepaid Items		$14,530.00	
Total Current Assets			$117,040.00
Fixed Assets			
151 Buildings	$250,000.00		
151A Accumulated Depreciatio	-$62,500.00	$187,500.00	
152 Land, Landscaping & Fenc	$25,000.00		
152A Accumulated Depreciati	-$2,500.00	$22,500.00	
153 Product Molds	$75,000.00		
153A Accumulated Depreciati	-$37,500.00	$37,500.00	
154 Office Equipment	$17,500.00		
154A Accumulated Depreciati	-$8,750.00	$8,750.00	
Total Fixed Assets			$256,250.00
Other Assets			
161 Incorporation Expenses		$15,000.00	
161A Accumulated Amortization		-$3,750.00	
Total Other Assets			$11,250.00
TOTAL ASSETS			$384,540.00

The following is the example of page 2 of the balance sheet, again utilizing some of the numbers in our chart of accounts example.

		Balance Sheet Example			
		As of October 31, 2005		2 of 2	
Liabilities					
Current Liabilities					
201 Accounts Payable - Trade		$22,920.00			
204 Notes Payable - Short Ter		$9,700.00			
Total Accounts & Notes			$32,620.00		
211 FICA Taxes Payable		$2,100.00			
212 Federal Withholding Taxes		$6,300.00			
213 State Withholding Taxes		$1,260.00			
216 State Sales Taxes Payable		$1,400.00			
217 Property Taxes Payable		$5,200.00			
Total Taxes Payable			$16,260.00		
221 Accrued Payroll		$2,000.00			
223 Health Insurance Payable		$1,300.00			
Total Payroll Items Payable			$3,300.00		
231 General Insurance Payable		$2,800.00			
232 Trip & Show Expenses Pay		$2,500.00			
Total Other Payable Items			$5,300.00		
Total Current Liabilities				$57,480.00	
Long Term Liabilities					
241 Notes Payable Bank			$97,000.00		
241A Less Short Term Portion			-$9,700.00		
Total Long Term Liabilities				$87,300.00	
Total Liabilities				$144,780.00	
Equity					
301 Capital Stock - Common			$180,000.00		
Retained Earnings			$59,760.00		
Total Equity				$239,760.00	
Total Liabilities & Equity				$384,540.00	

Review the two pages covered in this example balance sheet as if you are seeing the company's financial position for this period of time as one of its mangers.

THE INCOME STATEMENT

The income statement reflects the company's operational results for a certain period of time. GAAP advises that economic activity should be measured by matching the generated revenue to matched expenses for a fixed period of time.

Income Statement Example			
For the six months ending October 31, 2005			
Income			
401 - Product Sales			
401A - Sales - Product One		$216,820.00	
401B - Sales - Product Two		$141,310.00	
401F - Sales - All Other Products		$32,820.00	
Total Product Sales			$390,950.00
500 - Cost of Goods Sold			
501 - Material Costs		$175,927.50	
503 - Freight Out Costs		$46,914.00	
505 - Sales Discount Allowed		$3,909.50	
506 - Product Liability Insurance		$2,932.13	
Total Cost of Goods Sold			$229,683.13
Gross Profit			$161,266.88
Expenses			
600 - Warehouse Operating Expenses			
601 - Shipping Supplies		$1,200.00	
602 - Rent Warehouse		$3,000.00	
603 - Rent Equipment		$1,500.00	
604 - Equipment Repairs		$800.00	
605 - Building and Grounds Mainten		$900.00	
600 - Insurance		$2,100.00	
607 - Utilities		$1,272.00	
608 - Taxes - Personal Property		$1,200.00	
609 - Depreciation		$10,250.00	
Total Warehouse Operating Exppenses			$22,222.00
700 - Selling Expenses			
701 - Advertising		$15,483.25	
703 - Commissions		$5,864.25	
704 - Telephone		$1,296.00	
Total Selling Expenses			$22,643.50
800 - Administration Expenses			
801 - Salaries - Office		$21,500.00	
802 - Salaries - Officers		$47,000.00	
803 - Payroll Taxes Administration		$6,165.00	
804 - Interest Expense		$6,305.00	
805 - Insurance		$1,680.00	
806 - Supplies - Office		$1,250.00	
807 - Professional Fees		$3,000.00	
Total Administration Expenses			$86,900.00
Total Expenses			$131,765.50
Net Profit			$29,501.38

THE CASH FLOW STATEMENT

Another report that is a part of the financial statements is "The Statement of Cash Flows". The cash flow statement gives the manager the historical sequences (for a certain period of time), of revenue and assets changes, the investment activities, and the financing activities. The results are the increase or (decrease) in cash during the period covered.

Example of a Cash Flow Statement			
Cash Flows From Operating Activities			
Net Income			$29,501	
Accounts Receivable Increase		($9,000)	
Inventory Increase		($9,750)	
Prepaid Expenses Increase		($1,450)	
Depreciation Expense		$10,250	
Accounts Payable Increase		$8,000	
Accrued Expenses Increase		$1,200	
Income Tax Payable Increase		$1,000	$250	
Cash Flows From Operating Activities			$29,751
Cash Flows From Investing Activities			
Purchases of Property, Plant & Equipment			($37,500)
Cash Flows From Financing Activities			
Short-term Debt borrowing Increase		$2,000	
Long-term Debt borrowing Increase		$20,000	
Capital Stock Issue		$0	
Dividends Paid Stockholders		$0	
Cash Flows From Financing Activities			$22,000
Increase (Decrease) In Cash During Year			$14,251
Beginning Cash Balance			$6,599
Ending Cash Balance			$20,850

The above example gives you all of the possible ingredients of a cash flow statement. The example shows an increase in cash flow through operating activities by $29,751, a decrease in cash flow through investing in fixed assets by -$37,500, an increase in cash flow from financing activities by $22,000, for a net increase in cash of $14,251. It is good for you as a manager to see just where the money came from and where it went, and a cash flow statement included with your financial statements will give you that information.

FINANCIAL STATEMENT RATIOS

Financial statement ratios are mathematical comparisons that allow a manager to evaluate a company's performance or condition at a particular point in time. I have listed some of the key ratios used in evaluating companies today.

CURRENT RATIO

The current ratio for the balance sheet example shown earlier is the mathematical relationship of current assets to current liabilities:
Current assets $117,040 with current liabilities $57,480 = 2.04 which means for every $1 in current liabilities there is $2.04 in current assets. This indicates a good liquid position and management can quickly see what the company's liquidity is. Liquidity is assets than can turn quickly into cash to pay payables that are short term.

QUICK RATIO

The quick ratio is the relationship of assets that can be turned into cash within a matter of days to current liabilities. The quick ratio is the mathematical relationship of current assets minus Inventory to current liabilities. Current assets $117,040 − inventory $65,980 = $51,060 / current liabilities $57,480 = $.89. This would mean that for every $1 in current liabilities there is $.89 in quick assets. The company would only need to utilize the quick assets plus sell $6,420 of inventory to cover all current liabilities.

INVENTORY TURNOVER-COST OF GOODS PERSPECTIVE

This inventory turnover is the mathematical relationship of how many times the inventory turns in relationship to the cost of goods. The inventory to cost of goods relationship for the financial statement examples was: Cost of goods-material $175,927.50 to inventory $65,980 = 2.7 times for the six months covered by the statement. The cost of goods perspective represents the actual number of inventory turns, which is why accountants prefer this ratio.

INVENTORY TURNOVER-SALES PERSPECTIVE

This inventory turnover is the mathematical relationship of how many times the inventory turns in relationship to sales. The inventory to sales relationship for the financial statement examples was: total sales was $390,580 to inventory $65,980 = 5.9 turns for the six months covered by the statement. The sales perspective gives you an inflated picture as to the actual number of inventory turns in comparison to the cost of goods perspective.

ACCOUNTS RECEIVABLE TURNOVER

If the six months sales of $390,580 represent $65,097 in monthly sales, the $16,000 shown in accounts receivable trade on the example balance sheet would indicate accounts receivable turns of 4.06 times per month. These receivables would only be in house for seven days, indicating a very quick turnover.

DEBT-TO-EQUITY RATIO

Debt-to-equity ratio is the relationship between the long-term money provided by creditors and owner's equity. In the example shown the Debt-to-equity ratio is $97,000 in long term debt to $239,760 in owners equity which = 40.46. The debt-to-equity ratios for known companies are as follows:

Motorola 25.0
Pfizer 41.6
Texaco 59.9
Coca-Cola 82.7
Philip Morris 86.6

Any number under 50 is considered favorable.

PRICE-EARNINGS (P/E) RATIO

Price-earnings ratio (P/E) is the relationship of the stocks current market price compared to the earnings per share (EPS). To arrive at the P/E of a company you would divide the (EPS) earnings per share into the current market value. Example: If a company is trading at $38 per share and has earnings of $1.25 per share this would equal a P/E of 30.40. I have researched the fiscal year end P/E's of five companies to give you current examples: (high to low)

Corning	37.10
Adobe	34.30
Walgreen	30.00
PepsiCo	25.80
Boeing	25.20

In general, a high P/E suggests higher earnings growth in future periods when compared to like companies with lower P/E's. The P/E does show how much investors are willing to pay per dollar of earnings. In the examples above, Corning investors are willing to pay $37.10 per $1 of earnings, whereas Boeing investors are willing to pay $25.20 per $1 of earnings.

Income statement ratios usually are percentages of the total revenue, and the income statement example indicates the following computed percentages. Look for the footprints:

Cost of goods is computed as 58.75% of total product sales, yielding a 41.25% gross profit. Therefore, if the goal for this footprint was 40%, the results were right on. You then look at the various expense categories and see if the resulting totals for each fell within the projected ranges.

In the selling expenses area, advertising totaled close to 4% of sales; if your goal was 3%, this would indicate you over-spent your budget.

In the administration expenses the officers salaries are 12% of total sales, this percentage would possibly decrease as volume increases. Managers develop key expense items that they watch as each statement is presented, therefore giving them the opportunities to financially manager their company.

Managers trained to review their financial statements in this manner will develop their own guideline footprints to look for, and therefore enable them to make corrections quicker. This is the key; your ability to read the individual statements just like you are reading a book about the financial results for a specific period.

If you would like to research other ratios, I suggest checking out a book from the library that will give you information about how specific ratios are utilized. I have just touched on ratios here, but your accountant can prepare or suggest specific ratios for your particular company that will give you the comparative keys that you need to properly manage your company.

1.3 - ACCOUNTING FOOTPRINTS

I had advised you earlier that I would be giving you footprints to follow, and I have selected several footprints that should give you a much better understanding of where I'm coming from. We all need little hints or guides to keep us on track and to give us a better understanding of the subject matter that we are pursuing. You may find the following footprints helpful:

#1 – THE RULES FOOTPRINT –

When developing your accounting system, chart of accounts and financial statements, follow the rules, (GAAP) Generally Accepted Accounting Principles.

The generally accepted accounting principles have been established over the years to cover all areas of accounting; for our purposes in this book we will cover the rules pertaining to historical costs, accrual accounting, chart of accounts development and financial statements. This information can be reviewed in the basic accounting principles section.

#2 – HISTORICAL COSTS AND ACCRUAL ACCOUNTING FOOTPRINTS –

Historical Costs are the cost values entered through accounting entries. This gives the accounting records a consistency and reduces unnecessary adjustments as values change.

Accrual Accounting is when transactions completed may not require cash. This allows credit purchases or sales to be recorded, and therefore matching current revenue with current expenses.

Both historical costs and accrual accounting are accepted as – Generally Accepted Accounting Principles (GAAP), and allows comparisons between companies to be more realistic.

#3 – THE CHART OF ACCOUNTS FOOTPRINT –

The manager's participation in the development or improvement of the chart of accounts will give him a much better handle on the economic operations of his venture. As an example, the manager can select key accounts that he wants to glean information from and position them accordingly in the financial statements. A good example of this is shown in the advertising section of selling expenses; in the example chart of accounts, Basic Accounting Principles section. In this example, the manager wanted the advertising costs to show media, promotions, samples, direct mail, and agency costs as individual items. A good manager can glean a wealth of practical information from a well prepared set of financial statements, utilizing accounts that he had input in developing.

#4 – THE BALANCE SHEET NUMBERING SYSTEM FOOTPRINT –

The rules covering the numbering system for the balance sheet accounts in the chart of accounts gives the manager the quick keys as to the "why" of positioning of accounts.

An example of this in the Balance Sheet is as follows:

Current Assets

101 – Cash in Bank
  101A – Cash in Bank – Checking
  101B – Cash in Bank – Savings
  101C – Cash in Bank – Money Market
110 – Accounts Receivable – Trade
  110A – Allowance for Doubtful Accounts
111 – Accounts Receivable – Officers

112 – Accounts Receivable – Other
120 – Inventory Assets
    120A – Inventory Assets – Raw Material
    120B – Inventory Assets – Work in Process
    120C – Inventory Assets – Finished Goods
131 – Notes Receivable – Officers
132 – Notes Receivable – Other
140 – Prepaid Items
    140A – Prepaid Insurance
    140B – Prepaid Advertising
    140C – Prepaid Dues & Fees
    140D – Prepaid Office Supplies
    140E – Prepaid Trip & Show Expenses
    140F – Prepaid Postage

The lower numbers in the Balance Sheet 100-140, shown above, are the current asset accounts that either are already cash or will turn into cash in a short period of time.

The accounts 150-160, in the example chart of accounts, are the fixed and other asset accounts, and represent the longer term or other assets that are not considered current.

The accounts 201-232 represent the liabilities that must be paid the soonest, starting with the lowest number group, and the 240's in this case represent the long term debt.

The 300 accounts represent owner's equity which includes the capital stock and retained earnings accounts in the balance sheet.

The accounting formula written to include the account numbers would be:

Assets (100-160's) = Liabilities (201-240's) + Equity (300's)

This is a key footprint for the manager.

#5 – THE INCOME STATEMENT NUMBERING SYSTEM FOOTPRINT –

The rules covering the numbering system for the income statement accounts in the chart of accounts gives the manager the quick keys as to the "why" on positioning of accounts.

An example of this in the income statement is as follows:

400 – Income
    401 – Product Sales
        401A – Sales – Product One
        401B – Sales – Product Two
        401C – Sales – Product Three
        401D – Sales – Product Four
        401E – Sales – Product Five
        401F – Sales – All Other Products
    402 – Other Income
        402A – Interest Income
        402B – Lease & Rental Income
    402C – Miscellaneous Income

500 – Cost of Goods Sold

600 – Warehouse Operating Expenses

700 – Selling Expenses

800 – Administration Expenses

As you can see from the above income statement 400 accounts, the income accounts first cover the product sales accounts; the top selling products start with the lowest numbers. The next group of accounts shown covers the other income and miscellaneous income.

The balance of the income statement accounts (500's, 600's, 700's and 800's) will give the manager a quick understanding as to what account belongs in what group. You will quickly be able to see that a 700 account indicates selling expenses and #701-a, represents media advertising.

This positioning of accounts utilizing a numbering system over an extended period of time will give the manager a complete understanding of what each group means and where they belong on the income statement. Remember, the manager's key is to understand why the accounting system is set up with such a structured numerical method. The goal should be for the manager to be able to read his financial statements like a book, with complete understanding as to the "whys" behind the numbering system.

#6 – THE CASH FLOW STATEMENT - KEY ACTIVITIES FOOTPRINTS –

The cash flow statement covers all of the historical information relative to cash for a certain period of time. This historical information covers the revenue and asset changes, the investment activities and the financing activities within a certain fixed period of time (such as a quarter, six months, or year).

The cash flow statement is made up of three specific activities:

1. **Cash Flows from Operating Activities** (examples)
   Net Income
   Accounts Receivable increase or decrease
   Inventory increase or decrease
   Prepaid Expenses increase or decrease
   Depreciation Expenses

2. **Cash Flows from Investing Activities** (examples)
   Purchases of Property, Plant & Equipment

3. **Cash Flows from Financing Activities** (examples)
   Long Term Debt borrowing
   Capital Stock Issue

#7 – BALANCE SHEET RATIOS FOOTPRINTS –

The balance sheet ratios can give the manager a guide or comparison to previous periods and to like companies in their industry.

BALANCE SHEET RATIOS

Current Ratio

The current ratio in the balance sheet example shown earlier is the mathematical relationship of current assets to current liabilities.

Quick Ratio

The quick ratio is the relationship of assets that can be turned into cash within a matter of days to current liabilities. The quick ratio is the mathematical relationship of current assets minus inventory to current liabilities.

Inventory Turnover-Cost Of Goods Perspective

This inventory turnover is the mathematical relationship of how many times the inventory turns over in relationship to cost of goods.

Inventory Turnover-Sales Perspective

This inventory turnover is the mathematical relationship of how many times the inventory turns over in relationship to sales.

Accounts Receivable Turnover

This ratio represents the number of days it takes for the company's receivables to turn over.

Debt-to-Equity Ratio

Debt-to-equity ratio is the relationship between the long-term money provided by creditors and owner's equity.

The detail behind the above ratios can be found in the basic accounting principles section, but the important thing for you to remember is what these ratios mean, and the best application of them for your company.

Again, when a manager has background knowledge of a key, such as the above balance sheet ratios, it is so much easier to ask the right questions and to be "in the know" as to what the items shown on the company's balance sheet mean.

#8 – INCOME STATEMENT PERCENTAGE & RATIOS
FOOTPRINTS –

The income statement percentages are the ratios relative to the operational functions of the company, and this can give the manager a guide or comparison to previous periods, and to like companies in their same industry.

The most common income statement percentages are of individual items to gross sales as shown on our income statement example.

Total Product Sales	100.00%
Total Cost of Goods Sold	58.75%
Gross Profit	41.25%
Total Warehouse Operating Expense	5.68%
Total Selling Expense	5.79%
Total Administrative Expense	22.23%
Net Profit	7.55%

These income statement ratios are connected to an item in the balance sheet and give the manager comparisons of company to industry or period to period.

(ROI) Return on Investment – net income divided by owners' equity

(ROA) Return on Assets – net income divided by total assets / previous year.

(ROS) Return on Sales – net income divided by sales

The managers will rely on this information on a comparative basis to give them the positive or negative numbers from one period to another. The key will come when the manager develops the skills to utilize the information gleaned from these operational statements.

Are warehouse operating expenses in line, and what about the individual accounts within these expenses? How are the advertising expenses doing in comparison to the previous period? Are we spending too much money in the administrative expenses area?

The manager will have the tools to answer these questions and resolve problems by utilizing the information from the income statement percentages & ratios. These are the working footprint that every manager should utilize to monitor the company's operations.

#9 – What, Why, & When of Financial Statements Footprints –

(a) <u>What</u> is the balance sheet, <u>Why</u> is a snap-shot of the company's assets, liabilities, & owner's equity and <u>When</u> is a particular point in time and will be different the very next day.

(b) <u>What</u> is the income statement, <u>Why</u> is the company's operational results and <u>When</u> is for a certain period of time.

(c) <u>What</u> is the cash flow statement, <u>Why</u> is the historical sequences of revenue and assets changes, the investment activities, and the financing activities with the results being the increase or (decrease) in cash (where the cash came from and where it went) and <u>When</u> is for a certain period of time.

#10 – The T Account Footprint –

The T Account is simply a quick method of jotting down entries on a scratch pad, as explained earlier, either to show the detail of a transaction to someone else or to test an entry before formally recording it.

I classify the T account footprint as a tool for a manager to utilize when testing the effect of an entry before officially recording the information. I personally use T accounts frequently to explain an entry or the effect of an entry to a manager.

The key is to remember that the T represents the account; with the top line of the T showing the name of the account, the left side of the T being the debit, and the right side of the T being the credit. This will not help a manager if he hasn't learned the fact that assets have a normal debit balance and liabilities and owner's equity have normal credit balances. You just must think it out for simple tracing of an entry. Remember, debits increase asset accounts and credits decrease asset accounts, while credits increase liabilities and owner's equity and debits decrease liabilities and owner's equity.

You really have two choices – (1) re-read the area covering the T accounts in the Basic Accounting Principles section, or (2) ask your accountant. Hopefully I have explained the T account principle well enough for you to understand, because it really is a great tool. Go back and check out the scratch pad application that I had you do when explaining the T account in the Basic Accounting Principles section.

Section 2 – Business Examples

2.1   Types of Businesses

2.2   VIP Car Wash (Service)

2.3   Pasta-Ville Supreme

2.4   Compute-Tech Products and Services

2.5   Specialty Office Furniture Deluxe

2.6   Franchise Business Alternatives

2.1 - Types of Businesses

When an individual elects to form a new business he must choose the structure that will be the operating base, and should have an accountant advise them which would be best in their situation. Businesses can be formed in several different structures: sole proprietorship, partnership, "C" corporation, "S" corporation, or "LLC" limited liability corporation.

> ➢ **The sole proprietorship is the simplest in terms of organization, accounting, and reporting. As the title implies, one person owns and basically is the company.**
> ➢ **A general partnership (GP) is comprised of two or more owners who are liable for everything associated with the company. Usually and preferably, a partnership agreement is prepared to cover items that may come up during the development and operation of the company, such as: percentage of ownership, contribution of assets, and distribution of income.**
> ➢ **A limited partnership (LP) also is comprised of two or more owners with at least one of them as a general partner. These partners are investors only and cannot legally bind the entity in any way. The can supply input into the management decisions, but only as advice and not as the final decision.**
> ➢ **A corporation is a legal entity separate and apart from its owners, who are the stockholders. There are two types of corporations: privately held and publicly held. Privately held corporations are not traded on the stock market, whereas publicly held corporations have issued stock that can be traded.**
> ➢ **A "C" corporation means the corporation is taxed as a separate legal entity by the federal and state governments. A disadvantage to a "C" corporation is that its net income is taxed twice, at the corporate**

level and at the individual level of the stockholders, as dividends are considered income to them.

➢ An "S" corporation offers the same liability protection as the owners of a "C" corporation, yet the income is only taxed at the individual stockholders' taxation level.

➢ The "LLC" corporation is really a part limited partnership and part corporation. The owners of an "LLC" do have limited liability and can elect to have the same tax advantage of an "S" corporation. A "LLC" corporation could even be a sole proprietorship for individual liability protection.

The following list gives the reader different types of businesses that are common in the business world today.

Service
Service Only Business

The only commodity that they have is time and expertise in their field.

Examples:
     Accountant
     Lawyer
     Architect
     Consultant

Service with Goods

The revenue includes both time and material with an emphasis on their expertise and time.
Examples:
     Plumber
     Electrician
     Photographer
     Landscape Horticulturist

Food Service (private, chain, or franchise)

This is the most common small business to start up and the most likely to fail. The food service business requires a high level of service and a quality product. The food service business includes a component of retail sales with high employee costs.

Retail Sales

This group buys goods from a wholesale distributor or directly from the manufacturer for sale to the public. These operations have critical buying decisions requiring inventory controls, are very dependent on location, have lots of competitors, relatively fixed overhead costs, and reasonable employee expenses. This type of business could also be cyclical, dependent upon the type of goods sold. Again, this is a very common start-up business, and one that could fail easily. An individual starting this type of business should be very familiar with the products and risks.

Wholesale / Distribution

This is the middle-man supplier for retailers or manufacturers. They buy their goods in mass quantities worldwide, and supply these goods in smaller quantities to service and retail business and/or components for manufacturing.

The wholesale/distributor businesses operate on a mark-up margin that must cover all of their key costs such as: inventory, insurance, warehousing, labor and facility expenses, supplies, and database management. These types of business are very inventory intensive, and are continually dependent on their customer's business doing well, or always face the need to add to their customer base.

Manufacturing

This type of business often starts small with someone's idea of a better "mousetrap". A manufacturing business often will go through an explosive growth period in their early stages as they try to reach that profitable level through volume. They are built on the hope of volume sales, and reinvest profits toward new equipment, space, and payroll based on these volume projections. During these explosive growth periods these companies are at their most vulnerable stage.

Manufactured products, large and small, simple and complicated, cause the dynamics of manufacturing to be very complex. The establishment of distribution paths by management is very crucial to the success of a manufacturing company.

Manufacturing companies require a more complicated accounting system to give adequate information to management. Cost accounting becomes a very important part of the accounting system to assure that all material costs, production labor, and overhead expenses are accumulated relative to each product. Also, an adequate inventory control system must be in place to assure that materials will be available for each production cycle.

2.2 - VIP Car Wash

The purpose in this business review is to give you a general idea of what is involved in the operation of a car wash company, from the concept stages through financial information. I will be using a fictitious company name with this information to conceal the company's identity.

CONCEPT

VIP Car Wash developed a concept from the beginning to be a high quality car wash, with a membership program that would reward the car owner with special treatment and service. Two members of a family that had owned a car repair center for over 35 years felt the need for a high quality car wash service center catering to the VIP individuals. Two sons of the founder of the car repair center, with the blessings and financial assistance of their father, prepared a business plan for a car wash company called, VIP Car Wash. Originally, they had been washing and detailing cars for their father's customers in a small area within the car repair service center. The acceptance by their customers of the quality care the two sons had given their customers is what really prompted them to pursue the VIP Car Wash center, separately from their father's car repair center.

Lincoln, Nebraska, in Lancaster County was the city and county where Jim and Bill had decided to establish their VIP Car Wash. The population of Lincoln and Lancaster County was 230,000 when they were developing their car wash idea. Therefore, they felt this would easily support the venture and allow for expansion to other locations.

VIP Car Wash was developed with four basic areas of coverage:

1. **VIP membership for wash & wax**
2. **Regular car wash customers**
3. **Detailing customers**
4. **Quick Lube & Minor Repair Center**

The VIP membership would give the individual wash, wax, and vacuuming service for the members on a quarterly or annual time frame. The customer would have a sticker on their car that would indicate the type of service (wash only or wash and wax) and the expiration date. The customer could bring their car for car wash services as many times as they wanted over the life of the membership.

The regular car wash customer would be charged for the wash or wash/wax service each time that they came in. The regular customer could buy books for wash or wash/wax in 10 or 20 trip increments, at reduced rates.

The detailing customers would be charged a single total charge for compete detailing of their cars. Detailing would include: wash, vacuum, seat and mat wet vacuum service (with deep cleaning of the overhead and side panels), and hand waxing.

The quick lube and repair center would offer quick lube services, replace windshield wipers, broken head lights or tail lights, and have an established assortment of retail items relative to driver needs for cars. This could prove to be a nice profit center that supplied the customers with car-related items.

MARKETING

Jim and Bill's goals were to reach 50,000 individuals within realistic time frames by establishing one car wash near the original location in the center of Lincoln on East "O" Street, and two other locations, one south on Old Cheney Rd. and one north on 27th Street (north of Superior Street). The three locations would give the VIP Car Wash access to major traffic areas within the city of Lincoln.

VIP Car Wash's marketing approach:

> **To give exemplary customer service, assuring that their cars would be protected with the best in car care equipment and products.**
> **High quality washes for the discriminating customer.**

48

> **To establish a good customer base, the service must be convenient and fast respectively, with adequate hours of operation.**

Jim and Bill have established a very good working relationship with many of the established new and used car sales lots and their respective leasing departments. VIP has offered special rates when there have been commitments by these established car agencies.

The market trends have shown an increase in the high-end car owners to utilize the services of a reputable car washing service. The car washing market has shown a positive increase in the past five years, with a projected increase of approximately 4% per year over the next five years. Individuals that are living in apartments, town houses, and condominium units find it very inconvenient and often against the rules to wash their cars at these locations.

VIP Car Wash has a good start in marketing their services, and has been keeping a very positive approach in seeking new customers through the direct mail approach, utilizing flyers, color brochures used for hand outs at car agencies and mall locations, and newspaper advertising featuring the car care items.

VIP Car Wash has projected sales forecast for four additional years utilizing the last completed year of operations, 2004 as the base year. Refer to the sales and forecast chart on the next page.

VIP Car Wash
Sales & Forecast

	2004	2005	2006	2007	2008
Sales					
VIP Membership	$210,000	$218,400	$227,136	$243,036	$260,048
Regular CarWash	$182,500	$189,800	$197,392	$211,209	$225,994
Detailing	$37,500	$39,000	$40,560	$43,399	$46,437
Service & Retail	$161,500	$167,960	$174,678	$186,906	$199,989
Total Sales	**$591,500**	**$615,160**	**$639,766**	**$684,550**	**$732,469**

The above projections are based on an estimated 4% increase in sales in each car care category in the 2005 and 2006 years, and a 7% increase in the 2007 and 2008 years. VIP management feels that this is a minimum forecast, and should take into consideration the marketing plan for steady growth in their three locations.

TOWS Review

As I defined in the Glossary, the TOWS Review is utilized when making an analysis of a business, and consists of the following:

Threats – What known and unknown threats are against the business?

Opportunities – What opportunities appear to be available for the business?

Weaknesses – What weaknesses appear that could be a detriment to success?

Strengths – What are the obvious strengths of the business?

This type of review gives the manager a pattern to follow, and therefore forces him to review these four areas. When they concentrate on areas such as these, they can cover the basic areas that could determine the success or failure of the business.

Threats
- **Competition from local car wash companies.**
- **A slump in the general market.**
- **A tightening of the customer's spendable income.**

Opportunities
- **The population growth in the market area.**
- **The trend for the public to utilize car care more frequently.**
- **The increased number of apartments, town houses, and condominiums.**
- **An expanded market with their three locations.**

Weaknesses
- **Fuel costs affecting the driving public.**
- **The increased cost for individual services.**

> Marketing costs increasing faster than the demand.

Strengths
> Jim and Bill's contacts that have been established over the years.
> The development of customer loyalty through individual hands on treatment by the service personnel.
> The maintenance of the car care equipment that avoids damage to customer's cars.
> The quality of the car care supplies used.
> The showcase final results of the detailing operation.
> Quick lube services with customer comforts found in the lounges (free coffee and reduced prices on other concessions).

KEYS TO SUCCESS – FOOTPRINTS

1. VIP founders' knowledge of the market.

2. VIP founders' contacts developed over the years.

3. Quality of car care equipment and supplies used.

4. A marketing plan that covers four basic need areas for the customers (VIP service, regular car wash availability, detailing service, and quick lube services with quality car care products).

5.   The conveniences made available to the customer; long open times, quick turn around, and comfortable waiting room and customer lounge facility.

6.   Location conveniences: central (East "O" Street), south (Old Cheney Rd), and north (27th Street, North of Superior Street).

7.   Discount availability for car sales and lease agencies.

8.   Special discount books for multiple uses.

9.   To give exemplary customer service assuring them their cars would be protected with the best in car care equipment and products.

10.   High quality washes for the discriminating customer.

FINANCIAL INFORMATION

Break-even Analysis

I will develop a break-even analysis for VIP Car Wash based upon the following information:

The averages below are a combination of all services.

Average Per-Unit Revenue	$52
Average Per-Unit Variable Cost	$12
Estimated Monthly Fixed Cost	$8,200

VIP Car Wash
Break-even Analysis

Test	Units	Revenue	Variable	Fixed	Total Cost	Profit /-Loss
#1	200	$10,400	$2,400	$18,000	$20,400	-$10,000
#2	300	$15,600	$3,600	$18,000	$21,600	-$6,000
#3	400	$20,800	$4,800	$18,000	$22,800	-$2,000
#4	450	$23,400	$5,400	$18,000	$23,400	$0
#5	500	$26,000	$6,000	$18,000	$24,000	$2,000
#6	600	$31,200	$7,200	$18,000	$25,200	$6,000
#7	700	$36,400	$8,400	$18,000	$26,400	$10,000
#8	800	$41,600	$9,600	$18,000	$27,600	$14,000

The break-even analysis indicates that at the level of 450 revenue units, VIP Car Wash would be at the break-even level. I realize that the average per-unit revenue, the average per-unit variable cost, and the estimated monthly fixed cost could change from these estimates, but the study was based on the best available information at the time.

In 2004, the total sales were $591,500 for twelve months. Therefore if the average per unit revenue was $52, the monthly units for 2004 would be 948 (total 12 month sales = $591,500/12=$49,292/$52=948 units). As you can see by the chart above, 800 units with all of the factors shown would generate $14,000 in monthly profits. A break-even analysis of this type is a very good managerial tool and can be tweaked with new information as it becomes available. Utilizing this tool will help managers to "Cover Your Nut", therefore keeping on top of any major cost changes that come along.

My next study of the VIP Car Wash information will be the preparation of a sales and marketing expense forecast. Study the chart below, keeping in mind to observe the changes in marketing expenses utilizing a conservative sales increase.

VIP Car Wash
Sales & Marketing Expense Forecast

	2004	2005	2006	2007	2008
Sales					
VIP Membership	$210,000	$218,400	$227,136	$243,036	$260,048
Regular Car Wash	$182,500	$189,800	$197,392	$211,209	$225,994
Detailing	$37,500	$39,000	$40,560	$43,399	$46,437
Service & Retail	$161,500	$167,960	$174,678	$186,906	$199,989
Total Sales	$591,500	$615,160	$639,766	$684,550	$732,469
	100%	100%	100%	100%	100%
Cost of Goods					
VIP Member Cost	$52,500	$54,600	$56,784	$60,759	$65,012
Regular Car Wash	$42,888	$44,603	$46,387	$49,634	$53,109
Detailing	$8,625	$8,970	$9,329	$9,982	$10,681
Service & Retail	$37,145	$38,631	$40,176	$42,988	$45,998
Total Cost of Good	$141,158	$146,804	$152,676	$163,363	$174,799
	24%	24%	24%	24%	24%
Gross Profit	$450,343	$468,356	$487,090	$521,187	$557,670
	76%	76%	76%	76%	76%
Marketing Exp					
Direct Mail	$88,725	$92,274	$95,965	$102,683	$109,870
Media Advertising	$59,150	$61,516	$63,977	$68,455	$73,247
Promotional Exp	$29,575	$30,758	$31,988	$34,228	$36,623
Total	$177,450	$184,548	$191,930	$205,365	$219,741
	30%	30%	30%	30%	30%
Net	$272,893	$283,808	$295,161	$315,822	$337,929
	46%	46%	46%	46%	46%
Fixed Mo Costs	$98,400	$101,844	$105,409	$112,787	$120,682
	16%	16%	16%	16%	16%
Net Profit	$174,493	$181,964	$189,752	$203,035	$217,247
Percentage	30%	30%	30%	30%	30%

I have projected the cost of goods items to remain the same percentages of the individual sales categories as they were in the 2004 real information. Therefore, for the projection purposes, the gross profit percentages above remain the same.

I have also projected that the marketing expenses would remain the same percentages of the total sales; as they were in the 2004 real information. You can see that the marketing expense dollars are increasing from $177,450 in 2004 to $219,741 in 2008.

I have projected an increase in fixed monthly costs of 3 ½% for the years 2005 and 2006, and an increase of 7% for the years 2007 and 2008. Again, there is a large dollar increase in the fixed monthly costs, with percentages relative to total sales remaining the same.

Remember, when you are making a projection you can play with the "what if's" on paper to see how far you can go related to the sales, a lot easier and safer than if you were guessing in real time. Keeping tabs on how things are going through management financial statements gives you a heads-up when planning anything; marketing, equipment or facility expansion, and/or personnel additions.

The merit in spending the time to detail your projections should be obvious to you now. The base for reliable future projections can best be obtained by utilizing current income statements. Always rely on your financial statements to guide you in making your management decisions. If you keep the keys to success in front of you, and you are aware of the results of your operation through management financial statements, you will indeed have a better chance of making your business a success.

VIP Car Wash is a good example of a company made up of a combination of service with products, with the main ingredient being service. The car care products sold or used in this operation compliment the hands-on service care given to each customer. VIP Car Wash will continue to rely on repeat customers that come back because of the service given to them. Over half of the ten keys to success are related to service. Can you see the management footprints?

Footprints are very important for us to develop and to seek out when making an analysis of a company. Footprints should be an intentional thing a manager makes to insure that he is on top of the economical cycles of his company.

Can you see footprints in the operation that you are presently involved with, or can you see the merit in utilizing them in the future? Hopefully you can, because that is the reason for me supplying you with this type of information.

SUMMARY OF VIP CAR WASH

After the 2004 year of operation VIP Car Wash had a very positive balance sheet reflecting a positive current ratio, a positive return on investments, and a debt that was manageable. I did not print out the balance sheet or income statement individually for this business review, although the 2004 income statement was included as part of the sales and marketing expense forecast.

Management's success to this point in time has been due to their continuing desire to give their customers the best service possible, and their agreement to rely on financial statement input to guide them. The original founders established a management team of individuals who had been with them from the beginning. This team would meet monthly to review where they were and where they felt they should be heading. The team meetings from 2004 reflect the coordination of their efforts to cover all of the areas of the operation, with continuous plans to meet the demands of the future.

VIP's management was very careful to study every aspect of their operation to assure their success. Remember, our goal in going into any business is very simple, "to make money".

I challenge you readers to put some serious planning into any operation that you become a part of. If you are working for a company to gain experience before going on your own, give that company your time and energy to help them to become a better company, and therefore you a better manager.

2.3 - Pasta-Ville Supreme

The purpose in this business review is to give you a general idea of what is involved in the operation of a pasta restaurant, from the concept stages through financial information. I will be using a fictitious company name, with some of the information altered to conceal the company's identity.

Concept

Pasta-Ville Supreme's basic concept is to provide the public with a great pasta restaurant experience. The customer base is individuals, families, and take-out customers with discretionary income. They will do this by selling high quality, innovative products at a reasonable price, designing tasteful, convenient locations, and providing industry-benchmark customer service.

Pasta-Ville Supreme will be the leading gourmet pasta restaurant in this west coast city, with a rapidly developing consumer brand and growing customer base. The key will be to supply a line of innovative, premium pasta dishes which include: Almond Glaze on Smoked Salmon, Ham and Peas Linguini in an Alfredo Sauce, and Fresh Shrimp/or Lobster in a Marinara Sauce with Angel Hair Pasta. They also compliment their entrees with distinct soups and salads, desserts, and specialty beverages.

Marketing

The profile for Pasta-Ville Supreme's customer consists of the following geographic, demographic, and behavior factors. The twenty-five mile geographic target area includes a west coast city with a population of approximately 250,000. The restaurant's target population is estimated at 75,000 people aged 25-50; this is the segment that makes over 50% of this area's market. These target groups are young professionals who work close to the location, have attended college and/or graduate school, have an income over $45,000, eat out several times a week, and tend to patronize higher quality restaurants. When ordering at a restaurant, their health concerns are also taken into account.

As has been stated earlier, Pasta-Ville Supreme is providing its customers with a wide selection of high-quality pasta dishes, with soups and salads that are unique and pleasing in presentation; with additional offers of a wide selection of health- conscious choices, utilizing top-shelf ingredients.

The following benefits that the restaurant supplies are important to their customers:

> **Selection – A wide choice of pasta with soup and salad options.**
> **Accessibility – The customer can gain access to the restaurant with minimal waits.**
> **Customer service – The customer will be impressed with the level of attention that they receive.**
> **Competitive pricing – All products and services will be competitively priced, when compared with other high-end Italian restaurants.**

The market trend for restaurants in this time period is headed toward a more sophisticated customer. The restaurant patron today, relative to yesterday, is more sophisticated in a number of different ways:

> **Food quality – The preference for high-quality ingredients is increasing.**
> **Presentation and appearance – Patrons are beginning to understand and appreciate this part of their culinary experience.**
> **Health consciousness – As Americans in general are more cognizant of their health, they are requesting more healthy alternatives when they eat out. They recognize that an entrée can be quite tasty and still be reasonably good for you.**
> **Selections – People are demanding a larger selection of foods, and therefore appreciate a more complete menu.**

The global pasta market is nearing $10 billion dollars, and pasta sales are estimated to grow by at least 10% for several years. This growth is attributed to the same reasons stated above. The primary reason is that the health-conscious customer sees pasta as a healthy food because of its high percentage of carbohydrates relative to fat.

Another variable that is contributing to market growth in the restaurant business is an increase in the number of hours our demographic is working. Over the last five years the number of hours spent at work by our customer type has significantly increased. As the number of work hours increases, there is a high correlation of people that eat out at restaurants. This is intuitively explained by the fact that with a limited number of hours available each day, people have less time to prepare their meals, and eating out is one way to maximize their time.

TOWS REVIEW

As I defined in the Glossary, the TOWS Review is utilized when making an analysis of a business, and consists of the following:

Threats – What known and unknown threats are against the business?

Opportunities – What opportunities appear to be available for the business?

Weaknesses – What weaknesses appear that could be a detriment to success?

Strengths – What are the obvious strengths of the business?

This type of review gives the manager a pattern to follow, and therefore forces him to review these four areas. When we concentrate on areas such as these, we can cover the basic areas that could determine the success or failure of the business.

Threats
- **Competition from local restaurants that respond to Pasta-Ville Supreme's offerings.**
- **Gourmet pasta restaurant chains coming into this market.**

➤ A slump in the economy, reducing customer's disposable income spent on eating out.

Opportunities

➤ Growing market with a significant percentage of the target market still not aware that Pasta-Ville Supreme exists.

➤ Increasing sales opportunities in take-out business.

➤ The ability to spread overhead over multiple revenue centers.
(Pasta-Ville Supreme will be able to spread the management overhead costs among multiple stores, decreasing the fixed costs per store.)

Weaknesses

➤ A limited marketing budget to develop brand awareness.

➤ The struggle to continually appear to be cutting edge.

➤ The resources to compete with established chain pasta restaurants.

Strengths

➤ Offer high-quality ingredients with fast and frequent delivery schedules.

➤ Excellent staff who are highly trained and very customer attentive.

➤ Great retail space that is bright, colorful, clean, and located in an upscale mall, suburban neighborhood, or urban retail district.

➤ High customer loyalty among repeat customers.

➤ High-quality food offerings that exceed competitors' offerings in quality, presentation, and price.

KEYS TO SUCCESS

1 - Pasta-Ville Supreme has created gourmet pastas, soups and salads that are differentiated and superior to competitors. Customers can taste the quality and freshness of the product in every bite. The dough for the pasta is made with specialty Italian flour and the cheeses are all imported from Europe. The vegetables are organic and fresh with three shipments a week, and the meats and seafood are top-of-the-line selections.

2 - Pasta-Ville Supreme must maintain its mission to provide the finest pasta meal and dining experience for its customers. They exist to attract and maintain customers. When they adhere to this maxim, everything else will fall into place. Their services will exceed the expectations of their customers.

3 - The marketing strategy must be kept simple because of a limited budget. They will utilize radio (which often times is cheaper than print advertising), direct mail, banner ads, and inserts in the local paper. The radio ads likely may prove to be the most successful part of the campaign.

4 - The marketing objectives must be maintained as positive, with steady growth each month. Along with this, they must experience an increase in new customers who can be turned into long-term customers. Also, to assure their growth strategy they must add one additional store per year.

5 - The financial objectives should give them a growth spurt for several years, and give them a reduction in overhead per store through disciplined growth. They need to continue decreases in the variable costs associated with food production.

6 - Pata-Ville Supreme will target its marketing into three target populations:

> **Individuals – people that dine in by themselves.**
> **Families – a group of people, either friends or relatives dining together.**
> **Take-out – people that prefer to eat food in their own home or at a different location but want the quality of Pasta-Ville's food.**

Pasta-Ville Supreme has followed the above keys throughout the first year of operation and has been continuing the same keys in this second year. It has been very important to follow the steps mentioned to maintain the growth pattern and to reach out for expanded operations in the coming years. This target marketing must bring the message that Pasta-Ville Supreme offers the freshest, most creative, health conscious, reasonably priced gourmet pasta in this area. The campaign which includes the radio ads, the direct mail, the banner ads, and inserts in the local paper; will be complimented with public relations events with friends in local business organizations.

GENERAL REVIEW

Pasta-Ville Supreme has completed its first two years of operation and the restaurant has been well received. Marketing is now critical to its continued success and future profitability. The restaurant has been giving an extensive offering of gourmet pasta which includes fresh, creative, attractive pasta dishes, soups and salads, and specialty desserts to individuals, families, and take-out customers. The restaurant's use of homemade pasta, and fresh vegetables, along with premium meats, seafood and cheeses has gained them a very favorable reputation.

Pasta-Ville Supreme has accumulated very good information about their market, and knows a great deal about the common appetites of their most prized and loyal customers. This information gives the restaurant a better understanding of who is served, their specific needs, and how to better communicate with them.

SUMMARY

As I stated earlier, the purpose of this study of Pasta-Ville Supreme is to give you an idea of the many steps necessary to insure a successful operation. First, you want to lay out the company' concept in depth to assure that you will cover all bases. Next you want to plan your approach. As you read in the marketing area, this company highlighted several items that were keys to their marketing plan, selection, accessibility, customer service, competitive pricing, food quality, presentation/appearance, and health consciousness. All of those items were part of their marketing plan and because of their detailed planning; the footprints shown below are the <u>Keys to their Success:</u>

1. **The quality and freshness of the product.**

2. **The providing the finest pasta meal and dining experience.**

3. **The simple marketing strategy.**

4. **The skill of maintaining positive marketing objectives.**

5. **Reaching the financial objectives through disciplined growth and controlled expenses.**

6. **Marketing to the original groups (individuals, families, and take-outs).**

When you set out to make your own plans for your company; or to review the operations of an existing company, you cannot expect something to be a success just because you want it to happen that way; it requires planning and hard work (not, if I would have done this or that), you, must make it happen.

FINANCIAL INFORMATION

Break-even Analysis
To arrive at a break-even they must first arrive at several factors involved in the daily operational process:

➤ **The Average Per-Unit Revenue = $10.00.**
➤ **The Average Per-Unit Variable Cost = $4.50**
➤ **The Estimated Monthly Fixed Cost = $22,000**

Pasta-Ville Supreme
Break-even Analysis

Test	Units	Revenue	Variable	Fixed	Total Cost	Profit /-Loss
1st	1,200	$12,000	$5,400	$22,000	$27,400	-$15,400
2nd	2,200	$22,000	$9,900	$22,000	$31,900	-$9,900
3rd	3,200	$32,000	$14,400	$22,000	$36,400	-$4,400
4th	4,000	$40,000	$18,000	$22,000	$40,000	$0
5th	5,200	$52,000	$23,400	$22,000	$45,400	$6,600
6th	6,200	$62,000	$27,900	$22,000	$49,900	$12,100

As you can see by the chart above, they needed the sales level of 4,000 units to reach their break-even point, and from that point forward, the company would be profitable as long as they held their fixed costs at the $22,000 level. The study is based upon averages, and therefore if they had some differences in the per-unit revenue, the per-unit variable cost, or the estimated monthly fixed cost, they would show a difference in the break-even level. Management must keep on top of their costs and averages to provide break-even levels that they can rely upon.

SALES & MARKETING EXPENSE FORECAST

Pasta-Ville Supreme's first year reached the break-even point and the restaurant was headed toward a profitable second year. The second year indeed gives the restaurant a profit, and the following budget forecast is based upon the 2004 (second year) sales, direct cost, marketing expense, and estimated fixed costs. In the following budget forecast, the information was developed utilizing the assumptions of the following: 2005, a 25% increase, 2006, a 40% increase and 2007, a 50% increase. Management felt that the increases were very realistic, relative to their study of the area, and the potential customer base to draw from. The budget forecast was prepared with the increases, as well as an assumption that direct costs would stay at the same per-unit cost level. The budget has also made the assumptions regarding the relationship of marketing expense to sales, reflecting an increase in dollars, with a decrease in the cost percentage of total sales. The marketing expense factor was discussed earlier as being maintained with a conservative approach, to give the maximum utilization of the marketing dollar.

Pasta-Ville Supreme
Sales & Marketing Expense Forecast

	2004	2005	2006	2007
Sales		25.00%	40.00%	50.00%
Individuals	$103,710	$129,638	$181,493	$272,239
Families	$150,304	$187,880	$263,032	$394,548
Take Out	$25,401	$31,751	$44,452	$66,678
Total Sales	279,415	$349,269	$488,977	$733,465
Direct Cost				
Individuals	$46,669	$58,336	$81,671	$122,506
Families	$67,637	$84,546	$118,365	$177,547
Take Out	$11,431	$14,289	$20,004	$30,006
Total Direct	$125,737	$157,171	$220,040	$330,059
Gross Profit	$153,678	$192,098	$268,937	$403,406
	55.00%	55.00%	55.00%	55.00%
Marketing Expenses				
Radio Ads	$5,267	$5,605	$5,750	$11,002
Direct Mail	$11,704	$12,455	$13,547	$18,337
Other	$7,022	$7,473	$7,580	$7,335
Total Marke	$23,993	$25,533	$26,877	$36,673
	8.59%	7.31%	5.50%	5.00%
Profit After	$129,685	$166,565	$242,060	$366,732
	46.41%	47.69%	49.50%	50.00%
Fixed Costs	$22,000	$22,000	$25,000	$32,000
Profit After	$107,685	$144,565	$217,060	$334,732
	38.54%	41.39%	44.39%	45.64%

The budget also has increased the estimated fixed costs, which would reflect the increased stores opened in the area. The estimated fixed costs are the costs directly related to the fixed asset investments, made by the company with the increase required when new stores are added (costs covering buildings, furniture, and fixtures. Administrative costs were not included in this budget, but relative to the 2004 fiscal year they amounted to a total of $57,000. The administrative cost would not substantially increase until additional management would be required to cover the expansion of stores. Professional fees (legal and accounting) would probably have a slight increase relative to the complexity of the expansion. Interest would depend upon the need for additional borrowing to cover the expansion purchases. Administration costs should be a much smaller percentage of the total, but should be watched carefully to avoid unnecessary expenditures.

Let's look over this budget and glean what information we can out of it. First you will note the sales increases as shown by percentages under each year, second you will see that the direct cost has been maintained at the same level for each year in the budget, resulting in a flat 55% gross profit, third you will note that marketing expenses have changed at a variable rate with 2005, equaling 7%+ of sales, 2006 5 ½%, and 2007 (showing a sizeable dollar increase), but still reflecting a 5% of the sales rate.

Needless to say, as you can see the Pasta-Ville Supreme's profit after fixed costs in the year 2004 is very good, and the resulting financials should give the company strength to either attract new investors or make their credit line easier to establish.

When reviewing the financial information, you will find that I did not include a full profit and loss Statement, balance sheet, or statement of cash flow. In the studies of the individual companies, I have purposely left out these complete statements, because it will keep our concentration on the basic operational items rather than the individual statements. When you make the study of individual types of companies to help you decide which direction you would like to go in the business world, it is more important to review what makes them tick rather than getting into the nitty-gritty details of the financial statements. If we study the aspect of the break-even analysis and budget forecast we have established the foundation of what is necessary to "Cover Your Nut". I don't want to imply that the financial statements are not important for us to review; it is just a matter of what areas we want to cover and concentrate on.

A review of this type gives the reader the opportunity to see how a particular company "Covered Their Nut", through extensive planning and follow-up, from beginning to well after that first year of operation. As you reflect on the previous business reviews, and read the following business reviews, remember our purpose in this approach is to establish a pattern that you can follow for your own reviews. I want you to be able to apply the same types of analytic steps when you plan the particular company that you are interested in pursuing.

2.4 - COMPUTER-TECH PRODUCTS & SERVICES

The purpose in this business review is to give you a general idea of what is involved in the operation of a company that specializes in high-tech computer products; from the concept stages through financial information. I will be using a fictitious company name with this information to conceal the company's identity.

CONCEPT

Computer-Tech Products & Services is more than just another computer store; they do offer computers and other high-tech products for sale, and do have a service support department for the products they sell, but they also have a consulting and training department that covers all of the products that they sell. The founder of the company gained his experience through his employment at a major university. He spent 10 years working for a major university's computer support department. Through this work experience he was involved in all aspects of computer and high-tech equipment; from installation to repair, from software implementation to training, and finally in consulting with department heads regarding their equipment and software needs. The last couple of years at the university, he was elevated to the position of department manager. He therefore was able to supplement his hands-on computer equipment and software knowledge with managing, consulting, and training.

The founder decided to put his past ten years into the development of a company designed around the same perimeters as his department at the university, with the added ingredient of the profit motive. The company had also accumulated a core employee group through the founder's contacts developed over his years at the university. This group of employees would be responsible for managing their own profit centers, relative to their experiences. Computer-Tech Products & Services was developed with the following profit centers as their base:

1.   **Computer and high-tech equipment sales**
2.   **Computer and high-tech equipment service**
3.   **Computer software sales and training**
4.   **Computer and high-tech equipment consulting**

COMPUTER & HIGH-TECH EQUIPMENT SALES

This profit center is selling computer equipment both on the retail store level to individuals and on the corporate level to major companies. The equipment is from the major computer equipment manufacturers in the country, and features not only various brands of PC equipment but also Apple™ computer equipment. Monitors, printers, and other equipment would be included in this package of high-tech equipment.

COMPUTER & HIGH-TECH EQUIPMENT SERVICE

This profit center is capable of the complete service of all the equipment sold, as well as other computer equipment brought in by the customer. The repair service is supplying service to the individual customer's equipment, as well as for major companies and corporations. The employees in this department have received training certificates from the major computer equipment manufacturers, and therefore will be recommended as one of their service center providers.

COMPUTER SOFTWARE SALES AND TRAINING

The company supplies the best in both gaming and home use software, as well as very technical business software. The manager of this department has also received training certificates from the major software manufacturers, and therefore can both sell and train new and existing software. Regular training classes are made available to the public and to corporate groups, with computers and textbooks supplied by the company as part of the training tuition. The changes in operating systems and software programs make this service a very popular item.

COMPUTER & HIGH-TECH EQUIPMENT CONSULTING SERVICE

The founder had developed a very good relationship with many of the major computer manufacturers, and therefore was able to include consulting services for them. When the founder presented his consulting services idea to these manufacturers, they were more than happy to utilize this service for their products. Computer-Tech Products & Services is therefore established as the key computer equipment consulting service in the central United States.

The development of the cost center approach allows management to measure each department; not only how they contribute to the whole picture individually, but how they lead customers to the other departments. The company has developed an accounting system that gives them the necessary footprints to track both the successes and failures of each department.

Computer-Tech Products & Services not only include the sales of computers, software, and high-tech equipment, along with the service of all products that they sell, but also puts an emphasis on training. Training in the use of all computers and high-tech equipment and the software necessary to make operating systems work properly is a key to satisfied customers. Computer-Tech Products & Services consulting service is aimed at departments within individual companies and is conducted in their own space. The consulting service really centers on complete changes of either the computer hardware or major software package changes.

MARKETING

The population of the market area is approximately 350,000 people, with the customer potential of 100,000 individuals. The marketing goals for Computer-Tech Products & Services were to reach three distinct types of customers within the metro area and county where the store is located. The three types of customers are as follows:

> **Families with computer and high-tech equipment needs for home**

> Students with computer and high-tech equipment needs for school
> Companies and corporations with computer and high-tech equipment needs for work

The company's goals are to fulfill the needs of these three groups of people through top computer and high-tech lines of both hardware and software, with the following marketing approaches:

> To give each group of people professional and technical services above what is available anywhere else in the area.
> To assure the customers that their computer and high-tech equipment is the best available on the market.
> To supply each group with technical services for their equipment, with the repair costs kept reasonable, and with a short down-time.
> To provide professional training sessions for both hardware and software needs.
> To provide professional consulting services for customers owning small businesses or large corporations.

Computer-Tech Products & Services Company has accumulated a well- trained and technically oriented group of individuals that make up their management team. This team is responsible for the marketing of their products and/or services through marketing plans that cover the needs of the target groups. The marketing plans have consisted of specific methods of getting the word out to the public, such as:

> Media advertising – radio & newspapers (city and college)
> Direct mail – selected target groups
> Hardware and software company's recommendations

The media advertising consists of ads directed to families, students, and companies, with each separate ad covering the specific individual need. The direct mail pieces have been well-prepared to totally outline the departments available to meet the need of their customers.

The computer and high-tech companies have been eager to support the company with cooperative ad programs that feature both the products carried and Computer-Tech Products & Services Company.

Computer-Tech Products & Services Company has prepared a sales forecast starting with the base actual year of 2004. The projections cover the individual departments over the next four years, utilizing increase relative to population increases and market share.

Computer-Tech Products & Services Company
Sales Projections – 2005-2008
Base year 2004 (Actual)

	2004	2005	2006	2007	2008
Sales					
Computer and High-Tech Equipment Sales	$329,000	$342,160	$359,268	$380,824	$407,482
Computer and High-Tech Equipment Service	$178,000	$185,120	$194,376	$206,039	$220,461
Computer Software Sales and Training	$73,500	$77,175	$81,034	$85,085	$89,340
Computer and High-Tech Equipment Consult	$68,000	$72,080	$76,405	$80,989	$85,848
Total Sales	$648,500	$676,535	$711,083	$752,937	$803,131

Computer-Tech Products & Services Company's sales for 2004 reflected the following percentages of total sales (100%):

> **Computer and High-Tech Sales**   50.73%
> **Computer and High-Tech Service**   27.45%
> **Computer Software Sales and Service**   11.33%
> **Computer Consulting**   10.49%

The projections in the individual departments reflect different percentages of increase relative to the research done by the individual department heads. Even though the percentage increase was calculated separately for each department the only two departments that change are the last two (these changes were relatively small with the two of them still equaling the same percentage).

TOWS REVIEW

As I defined in the Glossary, the TOWS Review is utilized when making an analysis of a business, and consists of the following:

Threats – What known and unknown threats are against the business?

Opportunities – What opportunities appear to be available for the business?

Weaknesses – What weaknesses appear that could be a detriment to success?

Strengths – What are the obvious strengths of the business?

This type of review gives the manager a pattern to follow, and therefore forces him to review these four areas. When we concentrate on areas such as these, we can cover the basic areas that could determine the success or failure of the business.

The manager may want to add additional areas for expanding his review, but the four that I have selected cover a lot of ground. Any time that you look at the outside threats, opportunities, weaknesses, and strengths of a business you should arrive at a conclusion regarding your future possibilities, positive or negative.

TOWS REVIEW

Threats
- ➤ **Competition from smaller local computer stores.**
- ➤ **Competition from office supply chains.**
- ➤ **A tightening of the customer's spendable income.**

Opportunities
- ➤ **The population growth in the market area.**

> The continual changes in the computer industry.
> The trend for families to be more computer literate.
> The trend for students to rely on computers in their programs.
> The trend for corporations to hire consultants.

Weaknesses
> Internet purchases of computers and high-tech equipment.
> Increased costs for high-tech support services.
> Dependence on an ever changing industry.

Strengths
> The founder's experience and the team that he assembled.
> The contacts with major computer and high-tech companies.
> The abilities to cope with an ever changing industry
> The professionalism shown by the department leaders.

KEYS TO SUCCESS – FOOTPRINTS

1. The founder's university background and experience.

2. The development of a management team of experienced individuals.

3. The multi-coverage of all aspects of the computer industry (computer-sales, service, software, and consulting).

4. The assurance given their customers regarding

the quality of the computer equipment and software sold, as well as the service and training to back it up.

5. The consulting services available to corporations for selection of computers and software that fits their needs.

6. The ability to provide technical services for the equipment, keeping the costs as reasonable as possible.

7. The location central to the city and county therefore convenient to the customers.

8. The days and hours of operation; Monday through Saturday, 7:30 a.m. to 7:30 p.m.

9. Special offers for group training sessions.

10. Special pricing of equipment and software following consulting sessions.

FINANCIAL INFORMATION

Break-even Analysis
The break-even analysis for Computer-Tech Products & Services is based upon the following information:

Average Per-Unit Revenue	-	$325
Average Per-Unit Cost	-	$150
Estimated Monthly Fixed Cost	-	$19,150

Computer-Tech Products & Services
Break-even Analysis

Test	Units	Revenue	Variable	Fixed	Total Cost	Profit/Loss
# 1	50	$ 16,250	$ 7,500	$ 19,150	$ 26,650	-$ 10,400
# 2	75	$ 24,375	$ 11,250	$ 19,150	$ 30,400	-$ 6,025
# 3	100	$ 32,500	$ 15,000	$ 19,150	$ 34,150	-$ 1,650
# 4	110	$ 35,750	$ 16,500	$ 19,150	$ 35,650	$ 100
# 5	150	$ 48,750	$ 22,500	$ 19,150	$ 41,650	$ 7,100

The break-even analysis above indicates that at 110 units the company would have $100 profit, which is very close to the break-even point. I realize that this analysis is based upon averages and estimates, but it still gives them something to plan with. The goal is to establish the point where the company will "Cover the Nut" under different circumstances. Remember, you can easily make changes on paper that will give you a guide in planning the future of your company.

In the sales projections that we covered earlier you will note that the actual sales for 2004 were $648,500, and at $325 average per-unit revenue this would reflect just over 166 units per month. I purposely used simple, average per-unit revenue and cost dollar amounts for the simplicity of the study; whereas in a real life situation you would need to develop the four department revenue and cost averages and therefore show departmental break-even analysis.

Managers that utilize their financial tools, like the break-even analysis, will be continually monitoring the company's operation to assure a profit goal. Questions that the manager must answer are:

> **What is the average per-unit revenue in this current year?**
> **What is the average per-unit cost in this current year?**
> **Have the fixed costs changed from the original estimate?**

The manager's answers will give them the tools for future breakeven studies.

The following is the sales and marketing expense forecast for Computer-Tech Products & Services covering the actual information from 2004 and the projected information for 2005-2008.

Computer-Tech Products & Services
Sales & Marketing Expense Forecast

	2004	2005	2006	2007	2008
Sales					
Computer & High-Tech					
Equipment Sales	$329,000	$342,160	$359,268	$380,824	$407,482
Computer & High-Tech					
Equipment Service	$178,000	$185,120	$194,376	$206,039	$220,461
Computer Software	$73,500	$77,175	$81,034	$85,085	$89,340
Sales & Training					
Computer & High-Tech	$68,000	$72,080	$76,405	$80,989	$85,848
Equipment Consulting					
Total Sales	$648,500	$676,535	$711,083	$752,937	$803,131
Cost of Goods Sold					
Computer & High-Tech					
Equipment Sales	$151,834	$157,907	$165,802	$175,750	$188,053
Computer & High-Tech					
Equipment Service	$82,147	$85,433	$89,705	$95,087	$101,743
Computer Software					
Sales & Training	$33,920	$35,616	$37,397	$39,267	$41,230
Computer & High-Tech					
Equipment Consulting	$31,382	$33,265	$35,261	$37,376	$39,619
Total Cost of Goods	$299,283	$312,221	$328,165	$347,481	$370,645
Gross Profit	$349,217	$364,314	$382,918	$405,457	$432,486
Marketing Expenses					
Media Advertising	$32,425	$33,827	$35,554	$37,647	$40,157
Direct Mail	$19,455	$20,296	$21,332	$22,588	$24,094
Promotional Expenses	$6,485	$6,765	$7,111	$7,529	$8,031
Total Marketing Exp	$58,365	$60,888	$63,997	$67,764	$72,282
Net Profit	$290,852	$303,426	$318,921	$337,692	$360,204
Fixed Costs	$229,800	$229,800	$229,800	$229,800	$229,800
Net Profit	$61,052	$73,626	$89,121	$107,892	$130,404
	9.4%	10.9%	12.5%	14.3%	16.2%

I will now review the above sales and marketing expense forecast as a manager would make his review, starting with the actual year 2004:

1. **If the average per unit revenue was indeed $325, this would indicate that 1,995 units were sold in 2004, and with the projected sales increases (if the**

per-unit revenue stays the same), they would need to sell 2,471 units in 2008. The average unit cost of $150 would also indicate 1,995 units in 2004 and 2,471 units in 2008. The manager must verify his forecast each year, determining the average dollars for both revenue and cost, and then adjust his forecast accordingly. A good manager will continually tweak his forecast annually so that he can better judge where his marketing expenses will be.

2. Again, the marketing expenses are actual costs for 2004, and in this example each following year reflects the same percentage of Total Sales as shown:

Media advertising = 5% of Total Sales each year
Direct Mail = 3% of Total Sales each year
Promotional Expenses = 1% of Total Sales each year

The manager can also make the necessary adjustments in this area at the end of each year's operation. The forecast is a guide for the manager and must be adjusted annually to maintain cost controls.

The fixed costs in the example were actual costs for 2004, and reflect no change in the forecast for the following years. The manager must review these costs annually to assure that changes are truly reflected in future years.

SUMMARY

I have shown the reader in this individual business study the tools management can take advantage of while monitoring the operational cycles of his business. As I have stated in earlier studies, the financial statements (if developed as management statements) gives you a heads-up when planning anything.

Management's success in this particular business has been due to the foresight the founder has shown in the development of his management team. The individual managers that make up the team are totally committed to the success of their individual operation.

Which operation could the company do without? Time will tell if an individual department is truly contributing to the overall success of the company and when adjustments to the department need to be made.

It appears that management did plan for the need for each department, and indicated early on that the combination of them added to the overall success. If you have sales but don't provide service, your customer could go elsewhere. Software sales are definitely part of the picture, because as hardware changes, so does software, and if you leave one out, you wouldn't have the whole package. Software training just becomes a plus factor. The high-tech equipment consulting is a great door opener for the rest of the items, and therefore is complimenting the others in its process.

Again, you as readers of this book should be challenged to put these types of tools together when planning your individual operations. Remember, your keys to any success must include tools to insure that your company does "Cover Your Nut".

2.5 - SPECIALTY FURNITURE DELUXE

The purpose in this business review is to give you a general idea of what is involved in the operation of a furniture manufacturing company, from the concept stages through financial information. I will be using a fictitious company name with this information to conceal the company's identity.

CONCEPT

Two executives, having experienced the problems in finding a collection of top of the line furniture for their corporate office, home office, and home library, combined their knowledge and funds to form Specialty Furniture Deluxe. Specialty Furniture Deluxe focused the development of their line of furniture toward the high-end executive customers. The goal was to develop this line of furniture that would be unique to the marketplace and stand alone against competition from the international countries. The company has targeted the market where the demand for quality surpassed the demand for mass-produced furniture. The keys were to bring to market packages of furniture units to meet specific needs in the executive market place. These marketing packages were as follows: executive office furniture, executive home office/den furniture, and home library furniture.

This concentration in such a special area of the marketplace gives the Specialty Furniture Deluxe a limited but very strong section of the market. There was a major competitor, but the company's concentration in the three specific areas aimed at the high-end market gave them a strong base. The company expanded their market to not only high-end furniture stores, but office supply stores that would cater to the executive market.

MARKETING

The company's products are a combination of high quality furniture that fits an executive's needs for office furniture either at work or at home, with the addition of the executive home library furniture. The marketing strategy, therefore, is pointed directly to the executive manager or corporate officer, and will be a combination of a high quality catalog, direct mail, and an internet web site.

Obviously, the marketing would feature quality photos of this specialty furniture in whatever media they would select to showcase their products. Management decided early on that they would maintain quality, not only in their products, but in their approach to the marketplace. With this limited but lucrative field, quality must be the standard bearer. The executive market wants very fine furniture that features the latest innovations in office furniture, but still maintains the old-fashioned sense of fine woods and craftsman woodworking.

The executive will want his office, whether in a corporate tower or in his home, to be a showcase for him, and indicate his status and position; therefore, the company's marketing focus will be in the following areas:

- **Corporate offices – in the corporate tower or home office setting**
- **Home offices – in the executive's home setting**
- **Home libraries – in the executive's home setting**

As you can see, the company's marketing range is restricted to this executive market; therefore the presentation must emphasize quality furniture, which is an investment for the long term. The Bureau of Labor Statistics reports there are approximately 15 million executive, administrative, and managerial employees in the United States. The company developed a projection of potential based upon a very conservative portion of the market. The next step was to develop a market projection, starting with this potential, and adding growth for a five year period:

Specialty Furniture Deluxe
Projection of Potential Customers

Potential Customers	Growth	2004	2005	2006	2007	2008
Corporate Offices	7%	420	449	481	515	551
Home Offices	6%	125	133	140	149	158
Home Libraries	5%	50	53	55	58	61
Totals		595	634	676	721	769

The two founders had researched the needs for the three basic areas of potential customers, and found that the common thread was the desire to have quality furniture that would meet the demands of technology, but still would be ergonomically correct. The corporate offices were the real showcase area, therefore the furniture in this area must be of the highest quality in workmanship and materials. The corporate executive also wanted his home office and home library to feature the same high level of quality. This quality of workmanship and materials, therefore, became the bedrock for the company's furniture. and defined the marketing needs. The selected name gave the emphasis on what this furniture manufacturing company was all about, Specialty Furniture Deluxe.

The "baby-boomer" executive and the development of high-end corporate offices has become an important marketing trend for this company. Today's corporate offices are integrated with technology for muti-tasking executives in classical, high quality surroundings that require furniture that will complement this picture.

The development of technology in office equipment has made it possible for today's corporate executive to transfer files easily to laptop computers and to take the information with them, whether it is on a trip out of town or just home for the weekend. The pressures of today's business has put more demands on the corporate executive, therefore his office surroundings, both at the corporate office, or the home office must be comfortable and serviceable.

The corporate executive's home offices and libraries have increased over the past five years, with the trend to continue this increase at an accelerated pace. The home office has become an extension of the corporate office, and more executives are expanding their home libraries as a collection point for rare books, manuscripts, and paintings.

Specialty Furniture Deluxe has developed a demand for their products through various methods of promotion and advertising. The contacts that the two founders had developed over the years became the base for their original direct mail programs. The insertion of high quality ads in top corporate magazines became the standard for their media advertising. The promotional and advertising goals were maintained, utilizing high quality photographs, well-prepared copy that attracted the knowledgeable executive, and concentrated placement to reach the established executive, as well as the junior executives coming up.

TOWS REVIEW

Threats
- ➢ **Competition from local office equipment outlets**
- ➢ **Competition from local furniture outlets**
- ➢ **A slump in the general market effecting corporate executives**

Opportunities
- ➢ **The expansion and need for additional corporate offices**
- ➢ **The increase in "baby-boomer" executives**
- ➢ **The increased use of home office spaces**
- ➢ **The increase in collection of rare books, manuscripts, and paintings**

Weaknesses
- ➢ A reduction in corporate budgets
- ➢ The increased cost and availability of high quality material
- ➢ Increasing the demand sufficiently through projected advertising

Strengths
- ➢ The founders' contacts that were developed over the years
- ➢ The quality and workmanship of the furniture
- ➢ The developed customer loyalty among repeat customers
- ➢ The maintenance of the specific furniture style to meet this demanding market

KEYS TO SUCCESS – FOOTPRINTS

1. Specialty Furniture Deluxe's founders' knowledge of the market

2. The development of furniture that meets both the technological and quality demands of a very high-end market group.

3. A marketing plan that will show the current executives as well as the new group coming up that the furniture developed by Specialty Furniture Deluxe meets the demands of the corporate office, the home office, and even has something for the home library.

4. A tight, final inspection program for the finished furniture to assure that the quality is maintained, and that nothing reaches the market to tarnish the company's reputation.

5.　　A program for upgrading the corporate office furniture periodically with a trade-in allowance that invites continuing improvements.

6.　　A refurbishing program for the trade in furniture to supply new demands in other marketing areas.

7.　　Point system programs that would allow special discounts for the corporations that utilize the company's furniture in more than one of their corporate offices.

8.　　An interior decorator service for corporations to use at a limited cost for the development of the best application of the company's furniture package.

9.　　Assistance in planning for the establishment of both the home office and the home library.

10.　　Utilizing corporate customers in the Specialty Furniture Deluxe's advertising programs that will also benefit the customer.

FINANCIAL INFORMATION

Break-even Analysis
I have developed a break-even analysis for Specialty Furniture Deluxe based upon the following information:

Average per-unit revenue	= $4,300
Average per-unit variable cost	= $2,600
Estimated monthly fixed expenses	= $50,000

Specialty Furniture Deluxe
Break-even Analysis

Test	Units	Revenue	Variable	Fixed	Total Cost	Profit /-Loss
#1	100	$430,000	$258,000	$600,000	$858,000	-$428,000
#2	150	$645,000	$387,000	$600,000	$987,000	-$342,000
#3	200	$860,000	$516,000	$600,000	$1,116,000	-$256,000
#4	300	$1,290,000	$774,000	$600,000	$1,374,000	-$84,000
#5	350	$1,505,000	$903,000	$600,000	$1,503,000	$2,000
#6	500	$2,150,000	$1,290,000	$600,000	$1,890,000	$260,000
#7	600	$2,580,000	$1,548,000	$600,000	$2,148,000	$432,000

This break-even analysis was based upon estimated averages both in the combination of revenue items per unit, and variable costs per unit. I have also made assumptions regarding the fixed expenses staying the same.

Test #7 is very close to what the actual sales were in 2004 with the following unit breakdown:

Corporate office equipment	= 420 units
Home office equipment	= 125 units
Home library equipment	= 50 units
Total	= 595 units

FORECAST OF NET OPERATING INCOME AFTER MARKETING EXPENSES

The forecast of net operating income after marketing expenses has been developed, utilizing the first year of operation (being 2004) with the forecast covering: sales, cost of goods, marketing expenses, and estimated fixed expenses for the years 2005 through 2008. The revenue increase will be kept at a moderate level based upon the estimates for the company's market share, coupled with the expanded marketing efforts. The cost of goods will be maintained at the cost percentages reached in the 2004 year, and the marketing expenses will reflect the expansion in the marketing efforts.

The estimated fixed expenses will be related to property and equipment only, and indicate the need for expansion of the fixed assets as volume increases.

This forecast will indicate the combination of sales relative to the three areas: corporate office, with 7% increases, home office, with 6% increases, and home library, with 5% increases in revenue over the next four years. The estimated fixed expenses is shown with increases in the third and fourth years.

I have elected to include all administrative expenses in the fixed operating expense item that is show on the sales and marketing expense forecast. The idea behind this sales and marketing expense forecast is to show the effect in projected changes in the sales items related to the increases in the marketing expenses. I have shown an established increase in marketing expenses over the next four years of 5% each year.

Specialty Furniture Deluxe
Sales & Marketing Expense Forecast

	2004	2005	2006	2007	2008
Equip Sales					
Corporate Offic	$2,100,000	$2,247,000	$2,404,290	$2,572,590	$2,752,672
Home Office	$375,000	$397,500	$421,350	$446,631	$473,429
Home Library	$100,000	$105,000	$110,250	$115,763	$121,551
Total Sales	$2,575,000	$2,749,500	$2,935,890	$3,134,984	$3,347,651
Cost of Goods					
Corporate Offic	$1,260,000	$1,348,200	$1,442,574	$1,543,554	$1,651,603
Home Office	$217,500	$230,550	$244,383	$259,046	$274,589
Home Library	$55,000	$57,750	$60,638	$63,669	$66,853
Total Cost	$1,532,500	$1,636,500	$1,747,595	$1,866,270	$1,993,045
	60%	60%	60%	60%	60%
Gross Profit	$1,042,500	$1,113,000	$1,188,296	$1,268,714	$1,354,607
Marketing Exp					
Media Adv	$77,250	$86,609	$92,481	$98,752	$105,451
Color Catalogs	$51,500	$57,740	$61,654	$65,835	$70,301
Direct Mail	$38,625	$43,305	$46,240	$49,376	$52,726
Total Expense	$167,375	$187,653	$200,374	$213,963	$228,477
	7%	7%	7%	7%	7%
Operating Incon	$875,125	$925,347	$987,921	$1,054,752	$1,126,129
	34%	34%	34%	34%	34%
Fixed Expense	$600,000	$600,000	$650,000	$675,000	$675,000
	23%	22%	22%	22%	20%
Net Income	$275,125	$325,347	$337,921	$379,752	$451,129
Percentage	11%	12%	12%	12%	13%

All of the following percentages shown are compared to the total sales, which represents 100%.

The sales breakdown as a percentage of sales totals:

	2004	2008
Corporate office equipment	81.55%	82.22%
Home office equipment	14.56%	14.14%
Home library equipment	3.88%	3.63%

The sales percentage changes as the increase in each is different.

The cost of goods breakdown as a percentage of individual sales totals:

Corporate office equipment	60.00%
Home office equipment	58.00%
Home library equipment	55.00%

The marketing expenses as a percent of total sales:

	2004	2008
Media advertising	3.00%	3.15%
Color catalogs	2.00%	2.10%
Direct mail	1.50%	1.58%
Total expenses	6.50%	6.83%

The marketing expenses per each item remained the same percentages of total sales, plus, a 5% increase each year.

The fixed operating expenses for 2006, 2007 and 2008 increased, but percentages decreased: 2004=23.30%, 2005=21.82%, 2006=22.13%, 2007=21.53%, and 2008=20.16%

Footprints are very important for us to develop and to seek out when making an analysis of a company. Footprints should be an intentional thing a manager makes to insure that he is on top of the economical cycles of his company.

Looking back over companies that you have been involved with, can you see the management footprints? One of the main purposes of this book is giving the readers an insight into the footprints that will help them to "Cover Your Nut".

2.6 – Franchise Business Alternatives

I have given you the reviews of four distinct businesses; VIP Car Wash (a service business, Pasta-Ville Supreme (a food service business), Computer-Tech Products & Services (a combination service and sales business), and Specialty Office Furniture Deluxe (a manufacturing business).

General Information about Franchise Alternatives

I would now like to present the franchise business alternatives that are available to you. Interestingly enough, if you would go on the internet and do a search of franchise businesses, Google would give you 27,400,000 possibilities, and that can really be a bit overwhelming! Where do we start?

First, if you are really interested in a franchise business, more than likely it will be one that you personally know something about or have had a desire to own. You can do the internet search, trying to pin down the areas that you feel would be the best fit for you. You can attend a "Franchise Opportunities Show", as there are a number of them available across the country. The "Franchise Opportunities Shows" can be found in Las Vegas, San Diego, Pasadena, New Jersey, New York, or in Washington, DC. There are probably many other locations as well. Again, a Google search will give you locations and dates for the "Franchise Opportunities Shows", and it may be worth looking into and attending before you make your final decision. There are even companies that have been developed to assist you in financing your franchise investment. I gleaned two interesting statements from one of these franchise financing sites that are definitely worth quoting here:

1 - The number one reason people do not pursue their dreams of business ownership is a lack of financing. (You could say the same about any new business.)

2 - Buying a franchise is one of the biggest financial decisions you may ever make. (You also have heard this one before, your home and your car.)

Both of the above statements may be true and if you decide to go into a franchise business, financing does become a key, but there are many reasons why people want to go into a franchise business; owning a business they have always dreamed about, or gaining the support from companies that have the franchising system worked out, seem to be the main ones. Make sure that your dreams have been well thought out before making the leap into a franchise business of any kind, because it is a very important decision that you will be making, and one that can either be very rewarding or unfortunately disappointing. Use caution, and do your research into the franchise business you are interested in to assure success.

A franchise business allows an individual to share unique brand identification with other small businessmen and women, be privy to a tried and true method of doing business, and have a strong marketing program with a reliable support system. All of these items could be accomplished by an individual starting his own business, but usually a franchise system will reduce the risks, as others have already tested the market, and broken the ground in all of these areas. An individual can usually rely on the proven operating systems supplied by the franchise company, and can request information from individuals already operating the same franchise elsewhere in the country.

INFORMATION ABOUT SPECIFIC FRANCHISE SYSTEMS

I did go on the internet and researched some of the interesting franchise systems that are available, and I am listing some of the ones I felt would be recognizable to you. I have supplied you with fifty different franchise companies, and that is just the tip of the iceberg. Franchises are available in just about any type of business, so your challenge would be to select the ones that would be the best fit for you.

Key Franchises Available Today

1-800-Flowers	7-Eleven
A&W Restaurant	AAmco Transmissions
Ace Hardware	Ben & Jerry's Ice Cream
Bennigan's	Big Apple Bagels
Blimpie Sub's & Salads	Blind Shack
Captain D's Seafood	Carl's, Jr.
Country Kitchen	Discount Party Store
FastSigns	GNC Supplements
Golf USA	Haagen Daz's Ice Cream
Hardee's	Health & Fitness Center
Interstate Batteries	Java Jo'z
Jimmy Johns Sandwiches	Kentucky Fried Chicken
Kitchen Tune-Up	Kwick Kopy Business Center
Liberty Tax Service	Long John Silver's
Maaco Paint Center	Mac Tools
Meineke Car Care Center	Mentos Vending
Midas Muffler & Brakes	Party America
Pizza Inn	Purified Water to Go
Quizmos Subs	Ramada Inn
Red Bull Vending	Rent-a-Wreck
Service Master	Salad Creations
Snap-On Tools	Steak & Shake
Super Cuts	Subway
Sylvan Learning Center	Taco Bell
Taco John's	The Maids Home Service

Questions you need to resolve before investing in a franchise system

01 – Am I prepared to invest in and manage a franchise system?_

You need to be able to answer the same question that I asked you in the section covering Accounting & Business Questions/Answers.

Do I have what it takes to own/manage a small business?

> ➤ **Am I a self-starter?**
> ➤ **How good am I at making decisions?**
> ➤ **How well do I plan and organize?**
> ➤ **Am I willing to make sacrifices?**
> ➤ **How will I handle stress?**

Every one of these questions would be the same type of questions you would need answers to before starting a franchise system.

02 - What do I need to be successful in a franchise system?

You need the same basic items in a franchise that were covered in the same Accounting & Business Question/Answer section.

What do I need to succeed in a business?

The franchise system will actually supply you with three of the six items listed under the above question:

> ➤ **Sound management practices (you will still need to apply them yourself)**
> ➤ **Industry experience (they will give you training in this area)**
> ➤ **Technical support (normally a good franchise system will supply you with the needed support)**

03 – Will I be able to talk with other franchisees before investing in a franchise system?

The answer to this question is yes, but you should follow these guidelines when talking with the other owners.

You can require a list of franchisees before investing in the system but you must make sure that it isn't a list that was prescreened to say all of the positive things. It is not an impossible task to obtain a meaningful list of the franchisees; you just need to be persistent. There are franchise associations that can help and more than likely the company you are dealing with will give you the information needed.

04 - What types of franchise businesses are there?

When I researched the various franchise business on the internet, I was amazed at the number of different types of franchise businesses available. There were all types of franchise businesses found in my research; food services, general products, car-care products and services, self help services, and general personal services.

The following is a list of some of the categories I found listed in my internet search:

Automotive products and services
Business services
Business opportunities
Children's products and services
Cleaning and maintenance
Computer products and services
Internet services
Food products and services
Health and fitness
Home based business
Home services
Personnel and staffing
Retail business
Sports and recreation
Travel and tour services

As I advised you earlier, there are many opportunities available to you in the franchise business, but remember, you must apply the same kind of care and research to this type of business. Your goal in starting any business is "to make money", and the methods used to insure that you accomplish this goal is always the same, "Cover Your Nut" through research and serious planning.

Section 3 – Final Hints to Cover Your Nut

3.1 Accounting 101 Reviews

3.2 Business Examples Reviews

3.1 – ACCOUNTING 101 REVIEWS

In Section 1 – Accounting 101 I covered three basic areas:

1.1   **Accounting and business questions/answers**
1.2   **Basic accounting principles**
1.3   **Accounting footprints**

I want to leave you with some final hints to help you better understand the importance of having some knowledge of accounting when you seek your business ventures or goals. The repetition here is to put emphasis on items I consider to be most important for you to remember. I will cover highlights from each of the three sections with added hints for you to hone in on, (sharpen your skills and therefore become a better manager).

I am just high-lighting the key accounting and business questions/answers below, for your review.

01 – Do I have what it takes to own/manage a small business?
Since you will be your own most important employee, remember the questions you need to ask yourself.

> **Am I a self starter?**
> **How good am I at making decisions?**
> **How well do I plan and organize?**
> **Am I willing to make sacrifices?**
> **How will I handle stress?**

You should now understand how important it is to ask yourself these questions. Every one of these questions needs a positive answer for you to be a success.

04 – What do I need to succeed in a business?
The basic items you need for successes in a business:

> **Sound management practices**

97

- ➢ Industry experience
- ➢ Technical support
- ➢ Planning ability
- ➢ Investment capital
- ➢ Stamina / endurance

06 – How much money do I need to get started?

The money factor for a good start must not be overlooked, and you must have enough to cover the following:

- ➢ **The building and equipment needs (whether you lease or buy)**
- ➢ **The beginning inventory needs**
- ➢ **Finally, (and probably the one most overlooked), the money on hand to cover operating expenses for at least a year.**

Spend your time in planning this area very carefully, as your decisions made ahead of time will pay rewards to you in the long run, and could be the difference between success and failure.

10 – How do I set up my accounting & bookkeeping system?

The set up of your accounting system cannot be overlooked, and the following points need your total attention:

- ➢ **How will the records be used?**
- ➢ **How important is this information likely to be?**
- ➢ **Is the information available elsewhere?**
- ➢ **Will you need management or credit statements?**
- ➢ **What level of detail do you want to be tracked?**
- ➢ **How can the information be of most use to me?**

Your input in the beginning is so important to assure that the accounting system is really customized for your benefit. This will help you to become a better manager with the proper tools of accounting.

12 – What does "Cover Your Nut" mean?

The "Cover Your Nut" principle means to insure that your sales and revenue covers all of your costs and expenses over a given period of time.

Sales & Revenue	$10,000
Costs	5,000
Gross Profit	$ 5,000
Expenses	5,000
Net	- 0 –

The "Nut" in this example was the costs of $5,000 and the expenses of $5,000 therefore with Sales & Revenue of $10,000 did "Cover Your Nut". Please say to yourself; Yes, I now understand the "Cover Your Nut" principle.

BASIC ACCOUNTING PRINCIPLES

"Cover Your Nut"
➢ **Do you feel that accounting can and will give you the tools to show you if you are covering your business nut? Again, the answer should be YES!!!**

The Rules – GAAP

Generally Accepted Accounting Principles (GAAP) applied properly will give you a consistency that you need in your record keeping and Financial Statements.

The basic accounting formula to remember is: Assets = Liabilities + Owner's Equity. The following keys are the reasons for the basic rules:

➢ **Historical costs – a consistent application.**
➢ **Accrual accounting – matches income to expenses.**
➢ **Chart of accounts – a planned numbering system.**
➢ **The balance sheet – a snap shot of the company's assets, liabilities, and owner's equity at a specific point in time.**

➢ **The income statement – the company's operational results for a certain period of time (month, quarter, or year).**

➢ **The cash flow statement – where the money came from and where it went.**

Key accounts –

Cash accounts – reconcile monthly

Accounts receivable accounts – review aging report & establish bad debts reserve (standard journal entry)

Inventory accounts – establish inventory control system, consistently take physical inventories, (physical inventory teams), and reconcile the count to the inventory accounts.

Prepaid accounts – establish monthly standard journal entries.

Fixed Asset accounts – establish fixed asset worksheet covering purchase date, historical cost, life, depreciation method, and standard journal entries for depreciation.

Other Asset accounts – establish standard journal entries

Accounts Payable accounts – review monthly reports, to insure that payments are being made properly, and available discounts are taken, when the financial condition of the company allows. The importance of the company's credit record is obvious.

Notes Payable accounts – prepare a notes payable worksheets covering; name note payable to, inception date, interest rate, and monthly amortization schedules.

Capital Stock accounts – periodically check the stock books, and reconcile to stock accounts

Treasury Stock accounts – insure that proper documentation has been made, as stock is re-purchased by the company in the stock books

Paid-in Capital accounts – prepare a worksheet covering the transactions of the excess amounts paid for the stock; names, dates, and excess amounts paid.

Financial Statement Ratios

Financial statement ratios are mathematical comparisons that allow a manager to evaluate a company's performance or condition at a particular point in time.

- **Current ratio – current assets/current liabilities**
- **Quick ratio – current assets minus inventory/current liabilities**
- **Inventory turnover/cost of goods ratio – cost of goods/inventory**
- **Inventory turnover/sales ratio – sales/inventory**
- **Accounts receivable turnover ratio – credit sales/ accounts receivable**
- **Debt to equity ratio – long term debt/owner's equity**
- **Income statement ratios – percentages relative to revenue**
- **price/earnings ratios – market price relative to earnings**

ACCOUNTING FOOTPRINTS

Accounting footprints are the informational signs or guides for the manager to find his/her way around the accounting system and/or the financial statements.

#1- Follow the Rules (GAAP) Generally Accepted Accounting Principles

As has been shown to you throughout this book and many other reference books that you have read, the accounting principles rules are there for your benefit. Having a consistent set of rules gives the manager confidence that his comparisons follow the same rules as everyone in his like industry.

#2- Historical Costs & Accrual Accounting
Utilizing historical costs and accrual accounting allows comparisons between companies to be more realistic.

#3- Chart of accounts numbering system - Management's participation
The chart of accounts is the key to management financial statements. Management participation cannot be emphasized enough, when you participate in the birth of something, your understanding has increased accordingly.

#4- Balance Sheet Numbering System
The balance sheet numbering system gives the manager quick keys as to the liquidity of assets and the due dates of liabilities.

#5- Income statement numbering system
The income statement numbering system gives the manager quick keys as to the importance of the position of the account and the group they belong in.

#6- The cash flow statement activities

The cash flow statement covers the historical information relative to the revenue and asset activities, the investment activities, and the financing activities within a fixed period of time.

#7- Balance sheet ratios

The balance sheet ratios give the manager a guide or comparison to previous periods and to like companies in their industry.

#8- Income statement ratios

The income statement percentages are the ratios relative to the operational functions of the company, and can give the manager a guide or comparison to previous periods and to like companies.

#9- The What, Why, & Where of Financial Statements

The balance sheet is the what, a snap shot of the company's assets, liabilities and owner's equity is the why, and a definite point in time is the when.

The income statement is the what, the company's operational results is the why, and for a certain period of time is the when.

The cash flow statement is the what, the historical sequences of revenue and assets changes, the investment activities, and the financing activities is the why, and for a certain period of time is the when.

#10- The T account principle

The T account principle is simply a quick method of jotting down entries either to explain a transaction or to test an entry before formally recording it. Remember, the scratch pad T account gives you the quick review of the transaction, before actually posting it in the company's records.

3.2 – Business Examples Reviews

In the (2.1 – Types of Businesses) section I covered the various types of business formats available to you, with each having its unique format.

I am going to give you the list of these for your quick reference, and you can refer back to the 2.1 section for the complete information:

Sole proprietorship – one person

General partnership – two or more owners

Limited partnership – one general partner, with the others limited in liability

"C" corporation – a separate legal entity with shareholders

"S" corporation – separate legal entity with income taxed at individual levels

"LLC" corporation – combination of limited partnership and corporation

Not only are there the different legal formats for businesses there are basic differences in the reason for the business. Some of these are as follows:

Service –

Service only – accountant, lawyer, architect, etc.

Service with goods – plumber, electrician, photographer, etc.

Food Service –private, chain, or franchise

Retail Sales – private, chain, or franchise

Wholesale/distributor – buys in mass quantity and sells to retail or manufacturing

Manufacturing – buys raw material and makes products from it

In the balance of the business examples section I either covered the individual businesses or gave you information regarding the franchise type of business. The information supplied about the individual business covered the same type of outline:

Concept – this gives you, the reader, what was behind the development of the individual company.

When you are planning your business and set out to develop your business plan you must layout the concept of the business. Where is this business coming from?

Marketing – This also gives the reader basic marketing plans and follow-up. The marketing plans really will be the catalyst to make it happen in your business venture, therefore, the need for good planning with definite goals are obvious.

Keys to Success – The footprints that you can develop to monitor this success.

Financial Information – this is the area that you can glean the key "Cover Your Nut" reports, such as the break-even analysis report and the sales and marketing expenses forecast.

Summary – I have included a summary of each business example to highlight the keys. You need to plan well with your individual venture, and develop a summary of the keys to the business.

The businesses covered in this section are summarized as follows:

VIP Car Wash – This is an example of a service company that also sells products. I had a membership in this type of car wash. and had the advantage of being involved with the business for a number of years. This type of business is a very common example of a small business at its best; it involves all of the aspects of a "mom and pop" business that grows up.

Pasta-Ville Supreme's – This is an example of a private food service business developed with specialty products. Each of us can remember a restaurant that we have gone to like the one described here, and the reasons that we felt that it was unique. The analysis regarding this business gives you an insight as to what is really behind the development of a restaurant and what makes it succeed.

Computer-Tech Products – This is an example of how a retail store involved in common products and services can be developed into a successful operation. I experienced working with a business of this type and therefore was able to share the background and detailed planning to make a highly competitive business successful.

Specialty Furniture Deluxe – This is an example of a manufacturing operation and the necessary planning that goes with it, which is required to accomplish the goals of the business. I was involved with the development of a manufacturing company from the ground up, therefore the items covered are very realistic.

The most important thing that you should gain from the business examples presented in this book is the care you need to take in laying out the information about your potential or current company. The individual examples presented also give you an idea of how four different types of businesses have been developed, market their products, and insure positive financial results through operational forecasting and analysis.

Look around, I'm sure that you can see businesses that you are familiar with that would closely resemble that ones that I presented here. It is very important to remember what is behind the development of any business, and how you must be very prudent in your planning steps to be successful.

I LEAVE YOU WITH THE FOLLOWING:

Learn enough about the accounting information to successfully manage your potential or existing company. Your goal should be to understand the basics behind the accounting, not the need for attaining an accounting degree.

When you make your business plan, make sure that you develop it utilizing the steps necessary to cover all areas of the proposed business. Your business plan will be the resume of your new business; therefore, it deserves long term planning.

Select the business that you want to be involved in and then research every possible aspect of that business type before you jump in feet first. Your research can keep your head above water in such a competitive business atmosphere.

Finally, remember these basics:

1. **You can be a better manager through understanding all of the aspects, behind the scene.**
2. **The question you need to ask, and answer.**
3. **The footprints that you need to develop and follow.**

4. The developed ability that you need to read with understanding, the financial statements of your business.
5. Above all, the understanding of what "Cover Your Nut" truly means to you, personally.

WITHDRAWN

CPSIA information can be obtained at www.ICGtesting.com
Printed in the USA
LVOW061930030112

262215LV00007B/184/A